THE
POST-RACIAL NEGRO
GREEN BOOK

THE POST-RACIAL NEGRO GREEN BOOK

2017 EDITION

BROWN BIRD BOOKS

BROWN BIRD BOOKS

A traveler happened upon a small bird lying on its back in the road, its tiny claws pointing skyward. "Little sparrow," said the traveler, "what are you doing?"
"I have heard that the sky is going to fall," replied the bird.
"And you expect that your spindly legs will prevent this?"
The little brown bird was silent for a moment, and then it answered:
"One does what one can."

Brown Bird Books
P.O. Box 58404
New Orleans, LA 70158
www.brownbirdbooks.com

Copyright © 2017 by Brown Bird Books

All rights reserved. No part of this book may be used or reproduced in any manner whatsoever without written permission except in the case of brief quotations embodied in critical articles and reviews. For information, contact Brown Bird Books at P.O. Box 58404, New Orleans, LA 70158.

Printed in the United States of America

First edition published 2017
3 5 7 9 10 8 6 4

A Note on the Type:
The text of this book is set in Century Modern, a contemporary rendering of a 19th-century font style that was very common for the period. The font was designed by Stefan Cioroianu and is used by permission.

There will be a day sometime in the near future when this guide will not have to be published. That is when we as a race will have equal opportunities and privileges in the United States.

—The Negro Motorist Green Book, 1949

"The numerous racist incidents and the statistics cited by the Missouri Attorney General . . . are unconscionable and are simply unacceptable in a progressive society. We share the alarm and concern that Black individuals enjoying the highways, roads, and points of interest [in Missouri] may not be safe."

—Derrick Johnson, NAACP interim President and CEO, speaking on the NAACP-issued travel advisory for Missouri, June 7, 2017

CONTENTS

INTRODUCTION, 3
RACIAL BIAS IMPACT POINTS, 14
ABOUT THE DATA, 20

Alabama	21	Montana	104
Alaska	24	Nebraska	106
Arizona	25	Nevada	109
Arkansas	27	New Hampshire	112
California	30	New Jersey	114
Colorado	39	New Mexico	117
Connecticut	41	New York	118
D.C.	43	North Carolina	124
Delaware	44	North Dakota	131
Florida	46	Ohio	132
Georgia	54	Oklahoma	140
Hawaii	59	Oregon	144
Idaho	60	Pennsylvania	147
Illinois	61	Rhode Island	152
Indiana	68	South Carolina	154
Iowa	69	South Dakota	158
Kansas	71	Tennessee	159
Kentucky	74	Texas	165
Louisiana	76	Utah	175
Maine	82	Vermont	177
Maryland	83	Virginia	179
Massachusetts	86	Washington	183
Michigan	89	West Virginia	187
Minnesota	92	Wisconsin	189
Mississippi	95	Wyoming	192
Missouri	98		

DATA SOURCES, 194
#SayTheirNames INDEX, 195

INTRODUCTION

The Post-Racial Negro Green Book is a collection of occurrences, information, and data that document a pattern of racial bias against Black people in the 21st century. The events included took place between the years 2013 and 2016.

There is no commentary included in this book—just factual information. The format of the book, however, *is* commentary: it is based on the 20th-century *Negro Motorist Green Book*, which was published from 1936 to 1966. This segregation-era guide helped Black travelers find safe harbors and services in a United States that did not welcome them as equal citizens. The contents of the book you are holding right now indicate that we may not be as far removed from that United States as some of us think. The other influence for this volume is the book *100 Years of Lynching*, originally published in 1962 as an archive of newspaper stories documenting lynchings in America.

Just as there were far more lynchings than there were newspaper documentations of these lynchings, there is far more racism today than there is documentation of it. That is to say, neither *100 Years of Lynching* nor this book is exhaustive. In fact, the contents of this book, which were collected via a few simple internet keyword searches, could easily be expanded upon. And that still wouldn't account for the countless undocumented instances of Black people being called "nigger" each day—to their faces or behind their backs, being passed over for job interviews or promotions, being discouraged from goals because of assumptions about their race, being criminalized and harassed unjustly, and so on. What you see in this book is the tiniest tip of the hugest iceberg. In other words, like the original *Green Book*, this book documents a United States that does not welcome Black people as equal citizens.

WHAT THIS BOOK IS: NON-WOKE VERSION

About eighty years ago, a New York-area postman named Victor Green started producing *The Negro Motorist Green Book* to help Black travelers find accommodations and services in segregated America. My grandma would have been a teenager when publication of the book began, and she's still alive. That is to say, we're talking less than the span of a human lifetime from when Black people had to sit in separate areas until today. My grandmother is still alive, and so are people who supported racial segregation. And a lot of those people were both vehement and violent, as we know from photographs, footage, and other documentation of the era.

When the laws changed, what do you suppose happened to the vehement and the violent? Do you believe their opinions of Black people changed? Do you think they decided they had been wrong and adjusted their ideologies and beliefs? Of course not. They had to comply with new societal standards and laws publicly, but their feelings remained the same. And, like my grandmother, these people had children. And their children had children. And here we are today, in "post-racial" America, and it is still possible to fill a book with documented racism against Black people because, of course, it never went away.

Scratch the surface of America and you'll find racism. And this doesn't refer only to the descendants of people who celebrated lynchings or who screamed, cursed, spat upon, beat, and even murdered those fighting for civil rights. Also at issue are the people who felt quiet disdain toward the Negro, who went along with the new social order but still maintained their superiority—and their distance. All of these people, too, had children. And they, too, are America. The offspring of the vehement and the offspring of the quiet can be found making decisions in every role at every level of society, as the incidents in this book show. They are teachers, waitresses, judges, doctors, politicians, firemen, businesspeople, legislators, students, and—yes—police officers. So when you hear the collective voice of Black people saying that they are experiencing racial bias, what reason would you have to disbelieve it?

On another note, the label Black Lives Matter is no different than the labels Autism Awareness or Stand Up to Cancer. Yes, there are other disorders and diseases, but campaigning for one cause has never before been considered an act of war against the others. But you probably already knew that. You can care about Black lives, autism, cancer, police safety, heart disease, women's rights, and the price of tea in China—all at the same time.

Please consider this book a concentrated peek inside the overwhelmed subconscious of Black Americans. It's hard to find one who has had no exposure to racism, from being refused service at Denny's to being treated as a criminal simply based on skin color. It can be difficult to understand something that is not part of your lived experience, so please allow this book to provide you exposure to real-life occurrences that are happening to Black people every single day in "post-racial America."

WHAT THIS BOOK IS: WOKE VERSION

This is a history book. It is an archive. A time capsule. It is a means of preserving the seemingly countless incidents that have whizzed through your Facebook and Twitter feeds. The time between Trayvon Martin's death and now has been a whirlwind of awful news stories—sometimes accompanied by horrifying footage—and often the worst of it has gone unpunished. The justice system has failed, but be assured that memory will not.

This book is also a reference. A tool. As mentioned, there is no commentary included—just data and factual information. It is presented in a non-academic format with the express purpose of being accessible to a wide audience. Use it for research, discussions, proof, or even as a springboard for your own work.

In that regard, some notes about the contents:
- As mentioned above, this book is by no means exhaustive. It is a cursory review that easily could have been expanded.
- The incidents included have been verified or corroborated in some way. This required the exclusion of a great deal of personal testimony that, though likely valid, was unsupported in nature. As these types of narratives could have posed a credibility issue, they were omitted.
- The mere racial makeup of an incident (e.g., White police officer/Black victim) cannot and does not prove racism. Because of that, there may be incidents you were seeking that were omitted from this work.

- It is worth noting that, in some states, racism against Native people proved more prominent than racism against Blacks. South Dakota is a good example of this.
- Also worth noting: exclusion of 2017 incidents proved challenging because, even just at its halfway point, the year was rife with stories. A second edition of this book, with 2017 incidents alone, would not suffer for length.

WHAT THIS BOOK IS NOT

This is not a book about police brutality, and here is why:
(1) Police brutality is only one shade of the spectrum of American racism, which actually touches every possible area of life. This book is not limited to any one form of demonstrated racism.
(2) Police brutality is a universal issue, not a Black issue.

The Universal Nature of Police Brutality

In 2016, there were 963 people shot and killed by the police. Of that number, about 309 were black. For a group that is only about 14% of the population, African Americans made up 32% of police shootings. This is, indeed, a glaring disparity; however, using that disparity to make this a Black issue ignores the huge remainder of those people actually harmed by this behavior, who actually far outnumber Black victims. Police militarization, presidential encouragement of "roughness," and lack of accountability are issues that affect all of us—with, yes, a disproportionate share falling to Black people. But if you read through the accounts of these shootings, you will learn the following:

- **The stories don't really change across the races.** White people are also being shot for threatening with knives or BB guns, for failure to comply, for attempting to drive away, for acts committed while chemically impaired, and so on. They also

experience suicide by cop, accidental deaths (usually by car crash), medical crisis after tasing, and other fatalities. The following police narratives within the stories also repeat across racial lines:
- *I thought the suspect had a gun.*
- *The suspect was reaching for something.*
- *I feared for my life.*
- *The taser was ineffective.*
- *He or she matched the description of a suspect.*
- *He or she was threatening.*

- **More often than not, the person shot by police—regardless of race—was armed and posed a threat.** In the majority of these stories, the shooting victims of every ethnicity were actually engaging in criminal activity that endangered innocent people. And sometimes within these stories there are heroic interventions and lives saved by police officers. The heroism, too, crosses racial lines.

- **The population that is perhaps the most vulnerable of all crosses racial and even economic lines: the mentally ill.** The lack of patience, training, and competence to deal with this population has resulted in a frightening quantity of police shootings. Being a homeless, Black, mentally ill person seems by far the most dangerous possible combination when it comes to issues of police brutality.

Putting aside commonality across the races and focusing solely on police shootings of Black people involved in the commission of a crime, a different common thread also worthy of consideration emerges: in these incidents, the crimes being committed are more often than not economic in nature. When Black people have been shot by police, the stories rarely center around violent crimes like rape, battery, or murder. More often than not, when African Americans are actually valid perpetrators, they are fleeing something like a burglary, a robbery, a car theft, a shoplifting incident, writing bad checks, selling drugs, and so on. That said, the common denominator in these shootings is less skin color than it is poverty, which, particularly for Black people, tends to be passed down from generation to generation and is nearly impossible to escape based on a variety of systemic factors.

What Is and What Is Not Included
As mentioned above, there may be specific incidents you are seeking that are not included this book. Following is how inclusion was determined with regard to police brutality.

- Instances are *not* included if:
  - **There was no evidence to refute the officer's allegation.** In cases of he-said-she-said, this book errs on the side of exclusion.
  - **There was not enough information released to make any determination at all.** This isn't often the case, but at times there is little to no reporting on an incident, and in such cases, this book excludes rather than make assumptions.
  - **There isn't enough information to comfortably assert that race played a role.** Again, the existence of a White officer/Black victim dynamic is not, on its own, evidence of racism.

- Instances *are* included when:
  - **There was a White suspect who exhibited the same behavior for which Black people are consistently shot.** When White people are in possession of, reaching for, or even pointing a weapon at police yet are apprehended unharmed, it is difficult not to suspect racial bias.

- **There was no commission of crime or the crime was much too minor to warrant deadly force.** In many cases, this highlights a tendency to over-police and racially profile Black people.
- **The incident brings attention to issues that tend to affect Black people specifically.** This includes "broken windows" and other forms of overpolicing, patterns of systemic bias, and extreme disregard for life.

Evidence does corroborate that racial bias in policing is not imaginary. Police are sometimes overly aggressive toward Blacks, particularly males. Black people are indeed harassed for minor infractions and are likely to be the recipients of belittling or disrespectful conduct. But whether this type of behavior stems from personal racial attitudes or some other source, it doesn't exclusively result in police shootings; the picture is far larger than that. With regard to shootings, however, the conclusion here is this: Until the power of the other 68% of victims is harnessed, police brutality will (continue to) be dismissed as the ramblings of the race-obsessed and relegated to the division between Black lives and blue ones.

WHAT YOU CAN DO

The idea of taking on a problem as massive as racism should rightfully seem overwhelming. That said, the following suggestions and information are offered in hopes of breaking the problem down into more manageable components.

Acknowledge the full reality of the current situation. This book represents only a tiny fraction of the racism that is woven into the fabric of this country. Recognize and accept the severity of the problem.

Beware of scapegoating. Heaping all of the blame on a small segment of the population—whether it's Mexicans, the police, Muslims, or anyone else—has never resolved large-scale issues. Broaden your perspective.

Don't be a bystander. The events that are unfolding now are powerful and important. Raise your voice. Increase the numbers expressing discontent. Remember that events as critical as national elections can be won or lost due to apathy.

Start where you are. Do people indulge in racist commentary or behavior in your presence? Speak up. Let them know you don't share their beliefs—with or without further discussion. Are friends and family like-minded but standing on the sidelines? Be vocal about the issues, and try to find ways to engage them.

Find your niche. There are many ways—in addition to protesting—to make an impact. Start a petition, write letters, or provide support for others who *do* want to protest, such as offering to make signs or round up participants.

Join a local activism group. Ask around or check Facebook or Meetup for relevant groups. Can't find one? Start your own.

Learn about the issues. The battle against racial bias must be waged in many arenas—not just the streets. Review pages 14–18 for ideas about other points of entry. Many specialized organizations exist that can help you learn about and broach the issues presented on these pages. Look for these types of organizations working in your area.

Deepen your knowledge. Like the other contents of this book, the racial bias impact points on the following pages are just a hint of what's out there. Arm yourself with information—read the studies, find and review the data. Become an expert, and get involved.

Seek out workshops or organizations that can teach you activism and organizing strategies.

Concentrate your power. Choose a small issue—like a policy at your child's school that you recognize as affecting Black children disproportionately. Find others who agree, and rally your troops. A small victory could motivate you to bigger challenges.

Find places to divest and divert funding. Follow the money. Remember that race is a red herring and always has been—it is simply a means of dividing the bottom 90% to diffuse its power as the majority.

Share this book. Give it to the racism deniers in your life, to students, to anyone who needs to learn more or be challenged in his or her beliefs.

And, if all else fails: **consider relocating to Hawaii.**

RACIAL BIAS IMPACT POINTS

The data and findings on the following pages address the various junctures where outcomes for African Americans can be affected by race.

BIRTH/CHILDHOOD

One out of three Black children was living in poverty in 2015 compared to one in eight White children. Nearly one in six Black children was living in extreme poverty compared to one in 17 Whites. (Children's Defense Fund, 2016)

Roughly half of Black 3- and 4-year-olds were not enrolled in preschool programs. (Annie E. Casey Foundation, 2017)

Black children are the most likely to be in low-quality preschool programs. (Center for American Progress, 2016)

Children with no preschool or poor-quality preschool experience enter kindergarten a year or more behind their classmates. These children struggle to recover from this. (U.S. Department of Education, 2015)

Scores in reading and math were lowest for kindergartners in impoverished households and highest for those in households with incomes at least double the poverty level. (U.S. Department of Education, 2015)

Black boys as young as 10 are not seen as children the way their White peers are. Instead, they're perceived as much older than they are and as culpable. (American Psychological Association, 2014)

EDUCATION

When told to watch students in a video for disruption, teachers in a study watched the Black children. Though none of the children actually misbehaved, 42% of teachers identified the Black male child as problematic. (Yale Child Study Center, 2016)

Schools attended by Black children tend to lack quality resources, including experienced teachers, rigorous course offerings, and extracurricular activities. (U.S. Department of Education, 2014)

A study showed that when evaluating the same Black student, White teachers proved about 30% less likely than Black ones to predict the student would complete a four-year college degree and almost 40% less likely to expect him to graduate high school. (Johns Hopkins University, 2016)

Behavioral problems at school lead to criminalization for Black students and medical intervention for White students. (David M. Ramey, *Sociology of Education*, 2015)

Black students are suspended and expelled at nearly four times the rate of White students. (U.S. Department of Education, 2016)

Black youth are twice as likely as Whites to be arrested for crimes in school. (The Sentencing Project, 2015)

CRIMINAL JUSTICE / PRISON

A 2011 Bureau of Justice Statistics report showed that Black drivers are about 31% more likely to be pulled over by police than White drivers.

White people and Black people use marijuana at roughly equal rates, but Black people are 3.7 times more likely to be arrested for doing so. (American Civil Liberties Union, 2013)

Black men are nearly three times more likely to be killed by police intervention than White men. (*American Journal of Public Health*, 2016)

A 2010 report from the Pretrial Justice Institute revealed not only that pre-trial detention is more likely to be imposed on Black defendants than White ones but also that those who are detained pre-trial are more likely to be convicted and sentenced to longer prison terms.

A 2012 University of Michigan study found that prosecutors pursue mandatory minimum charges against Blacks about twice as often as they do against Whites who have committed similar crimes.

A 2009 Cornell Law study of a large sample of trial judges from around the country found that judges harbor implicit biases against Blacks and that these biases influence their judgment.

Despite the evidence that Whites and Blacks use drugs at roughly the same rate, Blacks are nearly four times as likely as Whites to be arrested for drug offenses and 2.5 times as likely to be arrested for drug possession. (Brookings Institution, 2015)

According to a 2009 report by The Sentencing Project, between 1995 and 2005, Blacks comprised about 13% of drug users but made up 36% of drug arrests and 46% of drug convictions.

Of the 225,242 people who were serving time in state prisons for drug offenses in 2011, Blacks made up 45% and Whites were only 30%. (Bureau of Justice Statistics)

The federal prison population is 35% Black. Half of federal prisoners are there for a drug offense. (Bureau of Justice Statistics, 2015)

Sentences imposed on Black males in the federal system are nearly 20% longer than those imposed on White males convicted of similar crimes. (U.S. Sentencing Commission, 2013)

State and local spending on prisons and jails has increased at triple the rate of funding for pre-K–12 public education in the last three decades. (U.S. Department of Education, 2016)

EMPLOYMENT/PAY

A 2003 field experiment showed significant racial discrimination against Blacks by sending out equivalent resumes with half given White-sounding names (Emily Walsh or Greg Baker) and half given Black-sounding ones (Lakisha Washington or Jamal Jones). White names received 50% more requests for interviews. (National Bureau of Economic Research)

A 2009 field experiment showed that Black applicants for low-wage jobs were less likely than equivalent White ones to be considered. Further, where the Black applicant had no criminal history and the White was just released from prison, the White candidate was still preferred. (*American Sociological Review*)

Black men's earnings are 73 cents for every dollar that White men are paid. For Black women, it's 65 cents to the dollar. The pay gap remains even where a college degree or better is considered, with Black men earning 80 cents to the dollar and Black women being paid 70 cents. (Pew Research Center, 2016)

Black households headed by a college-educated adult have a median income of $82,300 while comparable White households brought in $106,600. (U.S. Census Bureau, 2014)

HOUSING/WEALTH

Owning a home is the most common way for Americans to build wealth, and before 1968, discrimination gave Whites a huge head start. White homeownership is at 72%; the rate for Blacks is 42%. (U.S. Census Bureau, 2017)

Even with equivalent credit scores and other key risk factors, Black home buyers are 105% more likely to be given high-cost mortgages for home purchases. (National Bureau of Economic Research, 2016)

The median wealth of White households is 13 times the median wealth of Black households. (Pew Research Center, 2014)

Between 2004 and 2009, Bank of America and Wells Fargo's mortgage brokers charged higher fees and rates to Black borrowers than they did to White borrowers who posed the same credit risk. They also steered Black borrowers into more expensive subprime mortgages while comparable White borrowers received regular loans. This contributed to a

25% loss in wealth for Blacks across that time period—compared to only a 1% loss for Whites. (Pew Research Center, 2016)

The average Black household will need 228 years to match the wealth their White counterparts hold today. (Institute for Policy Studies, 2016)

ABOUT THE DATA

The data in this book are compiled from a variety of sources and encompass a four-year period—from 2013 to 2016. See the Data Sources section on page 194 for more information.

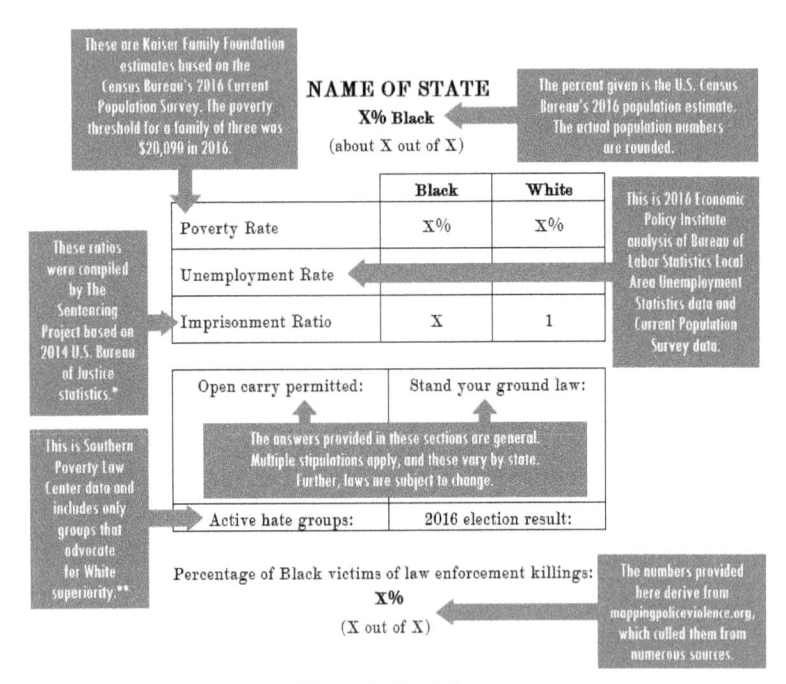

These are Kaiser Family Foundation estimates based on the Census Bureau's 2016 Current Population Survey. The poverty threshold for a family of three was $20,090 in 2016.

NAME OF STATE
X% Black
(about X out of X)

The percent given is the U.S. Census Bureau's 2016 population estimate. The actual population numbers are rounded.

	Black	White
Poverty Rate	X%	X%
Unemployment Rate		
Imprisonment Ratio	X	1

These ratios were compiled by The Sentencing Project based on 2014 U.S. Bureau of Justice statistics.*

This is 2016 Economic Policy Institute analysis of Bureau of Labor Statistics Local Area Unemployment Statistics data and Current Population Survey data.

Open carry permitted: | Stand your ground law:

The answers provided in these sections are general. Multiple stipulations apply, and these vary by state. Further, laws are subject to change.

Active hate groups: | 2016 election result:

This is Southern Poverty Law Center data and includes only groups that advocate for White superiority.**

Percentage of Black victims of law enforcement killings:
X%
(X out of X)

The numbers provided here derive from mappingpoliceviolence.org, which culled them from numerous sources.

Notable Incidents

These reflect the period of 2013 to 2016 only. All names in **bold print** represent Black people. Names written **THIS WAY** represent Black people who lost their lives due to the incident described.

Note: Data reported as N/A indicates a high margin of error in the estimate, which is likely a result of subgroups too small to provide a reliable sample size.

*Washington D.C. imprisonment ratio is based on October 2014 "DC Department of Corrections Facts and Figures" report.

**Included groups are the Ku Klux Klan, Neo-Confederates, Neo-Nazis, Skinheads, and White Nationalists.

ALABAMA
26.8% Black
(about 1,300,000 out of 4,800,000)

	Black	White
Poverty Rate	26%	12%
Unemployment Rate	10.3%	4.1%
Imprisonment Ratio	3.3	1

Open carry permitted: YES	Stand your ground law: YES
Active hate groups: 21	2016 election result: Republican

Percentage of Black victims of law enforcement killings (2013-16):
39.3%
(37 out of 94)

Notable Incidents

Upon catching a Black woman shoplifting, Victoria's Secret management ejected **Kimberly Houzah** and another Black woman from the store. Houzah, who did not know the thief, recorded a video of the incident. (December 2016)

A White police officer was fired after posting racist memes on Facebook, including one of First Lady Michelle Obama that featured text over a picture of Melania Trump reading, "Fluent in Slovenian, English, French, Serbian, and German" and text over Obama's picture that read "Fluent in Ghetto." Another meme showed Klansmen with a Confederate flag and read "The KKK is a hate group right? Isn't it about time we start being honest in America...and admit that #blacklivesmatter

is also a hate group?"
(November 2016)

A teacher at a Mobile, AL middle school was suspended after distributing a math test that included the following:
- "Tyrone knocked up 4 girls in the gang. There are 20 girls in his gang. What is the exact percentage of girls Tyrone knocked up?"
- "Leroy has 2 ounces of cocaine. If he sells an 8 ball to Antonio for $320 and 2 grams to Juan for $85 per gram, what is the street value of the rest of his hold?"
- "Dwayne pimps three ho's. If the price is $85 per trick, how many tricks per day must each ho turn to support Dwayne's $800 per day crack habit?"

(June 2016)

GREGORY GUNN (59) was walking home late at night in his neighborhood when an officer decided to execute a stop and frisk on him. According to the officer, Gunn ran; at this point, the officer tased Gunn three times and hit him with a baton. The officer claims that Gunn then wielded a weapon, causing him to discharge his firearm. Gunn was shot five times. Despite having turned his body camera on for previous incidents that night, the officer did not turn it on for this encounter. Further, Gunn's alleged weapon—a paint roller stick— was found not to bear Gunn's fingerprints. The officer was arrested, and a grand jury indicted him for murder.
(February 2016)

A White male fifth-grade teacher wore blackface to dress as Kanye West for Halloween. In apology, his wife stated, "Some of my husband's best friends are black. There was no racial intent whatsoever."
(October 2015)

Loyal White Knights Ku Klux Klan fliers were

distributed to homes. (March 2015 and October 2014)

Windows of a residence were broken and racist graffiti reading "move nigger now" was spray-painted on the garage door. (January 2015)

EMERSON CRAYTON, JR. (21) was the subject of a disturbance at a restaurant. When a summoned police officer arrived, Crayton was already in his car, as pointed out by the employee who made the call. The officer claimed that Crayton attempted to back over him, causing him to fear for his life and discharge his weapon, killing Crayton, who was unarmed. Though body camera footage clearly refuted this claim, a grand jury refused to hand down an indictment. (March 2014)

CAMERON MASSEY (26), a subject in a traffic stop, was shot multiple times by officers, who claimed he had posed a physical threat to them by dragging one of the officers with the car in his attempt to escape. Body camera footage proved this allegation false. No charges were filed against the officers. (October 2013)

RAY ANSON MITCHELL (37) was in his aunt's yard. She had called the police previously to remove her nephew, who suffered mental issues but was no danger, facts that she made clear to the officers. On the second occurrence, police entered the yard, and Mitchell ran. Officers gave chase and shot him to death, subsequently claiming that he had wrestled a taser from an officer and attempted to use it on them. Mitchell was unarmed. No charges were filed against the officers. (September 2013)

The EEOC brought a lawsuit against a Mobile-based insurance company after they offered a job to **Chastity Jones** and then told her she would have to cut her dredlocs to comply with its grooming policy, explaining that locs "tend to get messy." When Jones refused, the job offer was withdrawn. A federal appeals court ultimately ruled that banning employees from wearing their hair in dredlocs does not constitute racial profiling. (September 2013)

A 29-year-old White male was sentenced to 72 months in prison for attempting to hire Ku Klux Klan members to murder a Black neighbor. (August 2013)

Local Resources

Alabama Appleseed: alabamaappleseed.org, (334) 263-0086
Alabama NAACP: alnaacp.org, (256) 426-6406
American Civil Liberties Union of Alabama: aclualabama.org

ALASKA
3.9% Black
(about 29,000 out of 742,000)

	Black	White
Poverty Rate	n/a	6%
Unemployment Rate	n/a	5%
Imprisonment Ratio	3.8	1

Open carry permitted: YES	Stand your ground law: YES
Active hate groups: 0	2016 election result: Republican

Percentage of Black victims of law enforcement killings (2013-16):
11%
(2 out of 18)

Local Resources

Alaska State Commission for Human Rights: humanrights.alaska.gov
American Civil Liberties Union of Alaska: acluak.org, (907) 258-0044
Alaska NAACP: naacpaowsac.org; naacpanchorage.weebly.com

ARIZONA
4.8% Black
(about 332,000 out of 6,900,000)

	Black	White
Poverty Rate	n/a	9%
Unemployment Rate	9.8%	3.7%
Imprisonment Ratio	4.8	1

Open carry permitted: YES	Stand your ground law: YES
Active hate groups: 6	2016 election result: Republican

Percentage of Black victims of law enforcement killings (2013-16):
8.9%
(17 out of 191)

Notable Incidents

Racist fliers were posted on the campus of Arizona State University, including one that read "The age of white guilt is over!" (November 2016)

DALVIN HOLLINS (19) was fleeing a pharmacy robbery which he executed by holding a bag over his hand as pretense for having a gun. He was shot in the back and killed by a police officer whose body camera was turned off. Hollins was unarmed. The officer faced no charges. (July 2016)

Six White high school students posted a Snapchat using their lettered senior picture day shirts to spell out "NI**ER." (January 2016)

A White woman used Twitter to post a picture of herself and another White woman on a visit to a cotton farm. She captioned the picture, "Our inner nigger came out today." (October 2015)

RUMAIN BRISBON (34) fled when confronted by police investigating a tip about a drug deal. When caught, Brisbon struggled with the officer, who claimed Brisbon had his hand in a pocket where the officer felt an item he believed to be a gun. He shot Brisbon twice. The item was a bottle of oxycodone pills. (December 2014)

A White male member of a documented criminal street gang with White supremacist ideologies was arrested after yelling "white power" and "nigger" at a man, then attacking him with a bottle when confronted. The police report also indicated that the perpetrator said "Fuck niggers," "I don't give a fuck; I am a racist," and "I hate niggers." (August 2014)

MICHELLE CUSSEAUX (50) was the subject of mental health intervention. When police forced entry into her home, she threatened them with a hammer, and an officer shot her dead. The prosecutor's office refused to bring charges, but the officer was demoted after a disciplinary review. (August 2014)

A White man (Edward Carruth) provided extreme, physically violent resistance against police. He was tased several times but never shot. (April 2014)

A fraternity at Arizona State University hosted an "MLK Black Party" where they dressed in caricatures of Black people and used small watermelons as drinking cups. (January 2014)

ALEXANDER WILSON (16) was the subject of a stolen vehicle stop. Despite contradictory logistics, the officer claimed that Wilson attempted to run him over, so he fired, killing him. (April 2013)

Local Resources

American Civil Liberties Union of Arizona: acluaz.org
Arizona NAACP: arizonastateconferencenaacp.org
Attorney General: azag.gov/civil-rights

ARKANSAS
15.7% Black
(about 469,000 out of 3,000,000)

	Black	White
Poverty Rate	30%	12%
Unemployment Rate	9.8%	3.7%
Imprisonment Ratio	3.8	1

Open carry permitted: NO	Stand your ground law: NO
Active hate groups: 7	2016 election result: Republican

Percentage of Black victims of law enforcement killings (2013-16):
24.5%
(12 out of 49)

ARKANSAS (cont.)

Notable Incidents

Vandals spray-painted racial slurs onto the car of an African-American military veteran. (December 2016)

At a football game, students of a predominantly White high school yelled racial slurs while waving Trump paraphernalia at the visiting team of students from a Black high school. (November 2016)

There were calls for resignation after a Halloween costume photo surfaced showing a White school board member in Blevins, AR dressed in blackface, overalls, and a straw hat and holding a sign that read "BLAK LIVES MATTERS." He refused to resign and, as an elected official, could not be fired. When, shortly after, he was awarded an "outstanding board member" honor for completion of training, a crowd of supporters wore "I Stand with" shirts that bore his name. (November 2016)

> WE WILL NOT STAND FOR THESE NIGGERS ANY LONGER.
>
> ❖
>
> I WANT US ALL ON MAY 2 TO BAND TOGETHER AND BEAT US UP SOME NIGGERS, TOO. ...DON'T FORGET YOUR BASEBALL BATS.
>
> ❖
>
> I WANT TO SEE THE TREES RIDDLED WITH AS MUCH BLACK FRUIT AS THEY CAN HOLD.
>
> —ANONYMOUS

Researchers examined more than 2.4 million Twitter posts made on or near the campuses of 1,537 colleges and universities to determine the number of instances where tweets included racist language. By a large margin, the educational institution that had the highest percentage of tweets with racist terms was the University of Arkansas for Medical Sciences in Little Rock. (May 2016)

MICHAEL SABBIE (35) was arrested for issuing a threat to his wife. He was taken to a for-profit jail facility where he issued multiple requests for help due to trouble breathing. After a court appearance, Sabbie's request for a phone call was denied. A guard claimed he turned aggressively toward him, at which point several guards physically subdued and pepper sprayed him. In a nine-minute video of the incident, he repeats that he cannot breathe 19 times. His requests for help denied, he was left in a cell where he died overnight. (July 2015)

A WhitePrideRadio.com billboard was erected by the Knights Party. The site redirected to KKKRadio.com. (December 2014)

Fliers from the Traditionalist American Knights of the Ku Klux Klan were left in a neighborhood. (October 2014)

ROBERT STORAY (52), a disabled Army veteran, was escorted from a bus by a cop after causing a disturbance. He subsequently hit the officer with his walking cane, and the officer shot him to death. No charges were filed against the officer. (March 2014)

Local Resources

American Civil Liberties Union of Arkansas:
acluarkansas.org, (501) 374-2660
Arkansas NAACP: nwanaacp.org

CALIFORNIA
6.5% Black
(about 2,500,000 out of 39,000,000)

	Black	White
Poverty Rate	19%	9%
Unemployment Rate	10.9%	4.4%
Imprisonment Ratio	8.8	1

Open carry permitted: NO	Stand your ground law: NO
Active hate groups: 26	2016 election result: Democrat

Percentage of Black victims of law enforcement killings (2013-16):
16.2%
(124 out of 764)

Notable Incidents

Laguna Beach High School officials said they took disciplinary action toward five students they believed were involved in throwing a watermelon outside the home of a Black student—an incident the victim's parents labeled a hate crime. (December 2016)

WILLIAM SIMS (28) was brutally beaten and shot in the head by three White men who also robbed him. Audio recording revealed the men referring to Sims by the N-word prior to the attack. (November 2016)

The words "colored" and "whites" were scrawled above urinals at Monte Vista High School, which serves mostly White students. (November 2016)

A photo shared by California High School students on social

media showed urinals in one of the school's bathrooms that had been labeled with the words "colored" and "whites." The following week, graffiti that read "This bathroom is not to be used by fucking niggers" and "no niggers alowed [sic]" was found in a bathroom. (October 2016)

RICHARD GENE SWIHART (32), who was a known homeless citizen, was stopped for no known reason while riding a bicycle. An altercation ensued, and an officer alleged that Swihart tried to grab his gun, prompting the officer to shoot him. This particular narrative—"he was reaching for my gun"—is repeated throughout countless police encounters, many of which result from officers either accosting citizens without cause or escalating minor infractions. African Americans, the homeless, and the mentally ill prove particularly vulnerable to both the harassment and the narrative. [*See also* Brandon Glenn and Charly Keunang, below.] (August 2016)

JESSICA WILLIAMS (29) was spotted parked in a stolen car. When police approached, she tried to flee but crashed within 100 feet, wedging the car under a utility truck. An officer shot her while she was trying in vain to dislodge the car. She was neither armed nor driving toward him. The shooting brought to a head community sentiment regarding excessive use of force against people of color; the chief of police was forced to resign that same day. (May 2016)

Two 16-year-old White males sent a racially charged death threat to **Noah Porter**, their classmate at Central Catholic High School, via Snapchat. One of the boys pulled at a noose around his neck, saying, "You must die, motherfucker."

The scene then cuts to a handgun being fired. (April 2016)

While investigating sexual assault charges against a Chinese-American officer with the San Francisco Police Department, dozens of racist messages exchanged between four San Francisco Police Department officers were discovered. The Chinese-American officer made frequent use of the term "hak gwai," a Cantonese slur for Black people, at one point describing an incident as "a bunch of hock [sic] gwais shooting each other" and adding "too bad none of them died." In addition, the texts among the officers referred to Black people as "barbarians," "wild animals," "savages," and "niggers." There were also several pictures with racist captions, including one of an elderly man with the caption, "BACK IN MY DAY WE DIDN'T HAVE VIDEO GAMES. WE WENT OUTSIDE AND BEAT NIGGERS WITH STICKS." Another picture shows a White man spraying a Black child with a hose and is captioned "Go be a nigger somewhere else." (April 2016)

A blog post by a White mother of two biological daughters and two adopted Black sons came to the attention of alt-right members. The tweets she received as a result were laced with racial epithets and offensive comments deemed by a *New York Times* columnist as "shocking and unprintable." All of her social media sites were flooded with racist memes, including the posting of altered family photos with racist images over her son's face and a racist slogan superimposed. Many of the messages suggested that the Black children would harm the White ones. The harassment—which moved to 4Chan.org, where her address was published along with a photo of the outside of her house—was so bad that it was covered by several news outlets. (February 2016)

Years of media scrutiny prompted a State of California investigative report on the High Desert State Prison. Findings included open and widespread racism in which White inmates were given preferential treatment, including better job assignments, while Blacks inmates were referred to with racial epithets and disproportionately punished. (December 2015)

Hundreds of Berkeley High School students staged a walkout in response to racist messages posted after the school's website was breached. Comments including "Fuck all the niggers in the world," "KKK forever public lynching December 9th 2015," and "I hung a nigger by his neck in my backyard" were left on the library homepage. (November 2015)

The dean of students at Claremont McKenna College resigned after students criticized her response to a racist school climate—including students of color being spit on at parties, White students posing in racially offensive Halloween costumes, and vandalism of posters supporting Black Lives Matter. (November 2015)

There were three instances of racial comments being made regarding **Crecia Sims**, who was in her first year as principal at an elementary school. Two were included with an anonymous end-of-year staff survey. One said the school did not need a Black principal, and the other complained that Black students were not being suspended often enough. The third instance was a note left in the staff room after the weekly "collaboration" meeting. The note read, "Thanks, nigger for the collaboration." An NAACP spokesperson stated of the incident, "If you are bold enough to call the principal a nigger, we have no faith that you're able to dispense educational instructions in an equitable fashion that would be a benefit to our students." (August 2015)

In the Berkeley High School yearbook, someone changed the text regarding the majority Black- and Latino-populated Academy of Medicine and Public Service to state that it was focused on cultivating the "trash collators [sic] of tomorrow." (June 2015)

Deputy **Marcus Holton** was responding to a domestic disturbance when a mother and daughter refused to obey orders, in part due to Holton's race. His body camera captured the women shouting racial slurs at him. They were arrested and later sentenced to 30 days in jail for the language. (June 2015)

BRENDON GLENN (29) was the subject of a nuisance complaint. An altercation took place, and an officer later said that he saw Glenn's hand "on my partner's holster," which prompted him to shoot. But video from a security camera at a nearby bar showed that Glenn's hand was nowhere "on or near any portion" of the holster, nor did the officer's partner make "any statements or actions" suggesting Glenn was trying to take the gun. [*See also* Richard Gene Swihart, above, and Charly Keunang, below.] (May 2015)

A Black man was sitting in his running car in a parking lot when a White man suddenly opened the front passenger door. The man, a stranger to the victim, said that he had a gun and that the victim was going to die. As the victim got out of his car and started to flee, the White man uttered a racial slur and repeated the threat. The man was found and arrested on suspicion of criminal threats and a hate crime, both felonies. (April 2015)

A Black man was called "nigger" and told to "get his black ass off" a White man's property. The White man then beat him with a pipe. The former was arrested for assault with a hate crime enhancement. (April 2015)

Court filings from a federal investigation into police corruption revealed dozens of racist text messages exchanged by a group of 14 San Francisco Police Department officers. The messages included such statements as "all niggers must fucking hang," "cross burning lowers blood pressure," "niggers should be spayed," and "white power." In response to a text from a different SFPD officer about the promotion of a Black officer, an officer wrote: "Fuckin nigger." The evidence of bias by law enforcement officers was found to have put thousands of cases in question. (March 2015)

CHARLY KEUNANG (43) was being questioned by officers about a dispute between himself and another homeless man. He asked to explain several times, which elicited repeated threats from the officers of a tasing, to which Keunang ultimately acceded before crawling back into his tent. Cellphone video of the encounter picks up at Keunang being tased and ultimately subdued by four officers, at least one of whom continued directly deploying a taser while Keunang was on the ground. Another officer yelled "get off my gun" at least three times before Keunang was shot repeatedly. [*See also* Richard

Gene Swihart and Brandon Glenn, above.] (March 2015)

A White man was sentenced to 22 years and four months in prison after pleading no contest to felony charges of attempted murder and mayhem with a hate crime enhancement. The man, who had stabbed a Black man several times in the forehead with scissors in 2011, admitted that he committed the offenses "for the benefit of, at the direction of, and in association with" Neo-Nazi Skinheads, a White supremacist gang. (February 2015)

A White transient male in San Francisco yelled a racial slur at a 51-year-old Black man before striking him in the head with a pair of gardening shears and a hammer. (January 2015)

Fliers from the Loyal White Knights of the Ku Klux Klan were distributed in a neighborhood. This is the same chapter responsible for a February 2016 Anaheim rally that ended in violence. (January 2015)

The final member of a trio of assailants was sentenced for a 2011 assault on a mixed-race couple. The men smashed the windshield of the couple's car, kicked the woman in the chest, and battered the man. Each of the assailants has White supremacist tattoos, and all admitted that their actions were based on race. (December 2014)

A noose was found hanging at the Berkeley High School campus. (October 2014)

EZELL FORD (25) was unarmed and simply walking down the street in his own neighborhood when he was confronted by police officers. Ford, who suffered from mental illness, was shot three times in the ensuing struggle. (August 2014)

An Asian man (Lance Tamayo) waved his gun around and pointing it directly at men, women, children, and some police officers in a public park. Police engaged in an hour-long negotiation with him before shooting him once in the stomach. He survived and was later sentenced to 180 days in jail. (August 2014)

Fliers were distributed by the Loyal White Knights of the Ku Klux Klan. (July 2014)

Cell phone video showed a homeless, unarmed Black woman, **Marlene Pinnock**, being savagely beaten by a White California Highway Patrol officer. An officer had been summoned based on her walking along the roadway. (July 2014)

TOMMY YANCY, JR. (32) was pulled over for not having a front license plate. Bystander video, which picks up after the initial altercation with the officers, begins with Yancy being tased while handcuffed on the ground as an officer jumps on him with his knees. Ultimately, he was beaten to death by five California Highway Patrol officers. A woman in the background of the video can be heard screaming, "I think that is too much excessive!" (May 2014)

A Black woman passed by a group of men on her way into a bar. One of the men commented about why "colored people" were allowed in the bar. The woman confronted the men about the remark and then walked away. When she went to smoke a cigarette later, a pair of White men punched and kicked her repeatedly until she was unconscious. The men—a father and son pair— were found and arrested. (December 2013)

When **Donald Williams, Jr.** was a freshman at San Jose State University, he was assigned three White male roommates. That semester, the roommates engaged in bullying that included, among other things, writing the N-word on a whiteboard, draping the Confederate flag on the wall of their common study area, and wrestling Williams to the ground and fastening a bike lock around his neck. The roommates were expelled and faced criminal charges. (November 2013)

> **We don't want any more worthless, drains on society, ill-mannered, disrespectful niggers in this town.**
> —anonymous letter writer

Rocks in the shape of a swastika were left in the front yard of Councilwoman **Nancy Young**. (July 2013)

TOUSSAINT HARRISON (34) became engaged in a verbal altercation with a White man. Harrison had disengaged, departing on his bicycle, but the man followed him in a truck and ran him over in a parking lot. He then got out of the truck and began kicking Harrison in the head as he lay on the ground. Witnesses stated that the man used racial slurs in the commission of the crime. He also used them in the patrol car, after he was arrested, in addition to saying, "Just because we got Obama for a president these people think they are real special." (June 2013)

Local Resources

American Civil Liberties Union of Northern California: aclunc.org
American Civil Liberties Union of Southern California: aclusocal.org
Attorney General: oag.ca.gov/civil
California NAACP: ca-naacp.org

COLORADO
4.5% Black
(about 249,000 out of 5,500,000)

	Black	White
Poverty Rate	n/a	7%
Unemployment Rate	n/a	3.3%
Imprisonment Ratio	7.3	1

Open carry permitted: YES	Stand your ground law: NO
Active hate groups: 4	2016 election result: Democrat

Percentage of Black victims of law enforcement killings (2013-16):
10.6%
(11 out of 104)

Notable Incidents

A White doctor faced disciplinary action after using Facebook to post an unflattering photo of Michelle Obama with the comment "Monkey face and poor ebonic English!!! There! I feel better and am still not racist!!! Just calling it like it is!" (December 2016)

Denver Broncos player **Brandon Marshall**, who had been taking a knee during the national anthem, received a hand-written letter that read:

HELLO MR MARSHALL

HOW ARE YOU? YOU ARE A GREAT FOOTBALL PLAYER MR MARSHALL, NO YOU ARE NOT! YOU ARE A WORTHLESS FUCKING NIGGER WHO IS A SPOILED FUCKING JIGABOO!! IF YOU ARE SOOO UNHAPPY WITH AMERICA, TURN IN YOUR "MILLIONS" AND MOVE BACK TO THE JUNGLE, YOU FUCKING GORILLA

MONKEY!! WE HATE YOU AND YOUR "KIND" OF NIGGERS!! YOU BLACK FUCKING PORCH MONKEY YOUR NAME SHOULD BE SASABO. YOUR TIME IS COMING, WATCH OUT NIGGER!!

GO BACK TO AFRICA YOU "MUD PUPPET"
(December 2016)

As **Deon Jones** of Aurora, CO sat legally parked in his car in Denver, waiting for a friend, a cop ran his plate. The plates were clean but identified Jones as a non-Denver resident, which prompted the officer to state "he doesn't belong here" and to accost him. When Jones refused to exit the vehicle, body camera footage shows that he was held at gunpoint, thrown to the ground, and arrested without probable cause. A lawsuit is pending. (April 2016)

MICHAEL LEE MARSHALL (50) was homeless and suffered from schizophrenia. While detained for a minor charge, he was nervously pacing, which prompted three sheriff's deputies to restrain him into unconsciousness. He died after nine days on life support. The officers faced no charges. (November 2015)

A Black man and his brother were driving a block away from their home in a predominantly white neighborhood. Police pulled them over, held them at taser and gunpoint, handcuffed them, searched them, and detained them. One of the brothers recorded the incident with his cell phone. The ACLU filed a lawsuit on the brothers' behalf, and the police department settled. (March 2015)

NAESCHYLUS VINZANT (37) was a parolee who had removed his ankle monitor. Upon being confronted by a SWAT officer, Vinzant allegedly assumed a fighting stance. The officer shot him in the chest, killing him. Vinzant was unarmed. A grand jury refused indictment. (March 2015)

Three Black men were in a parking lot when a White man in a car pulled over and called out an expletive and the N-word, according to court records. The men argued with the driver, who drove away but came back—stating, "I told you mother fucking niggers I wasn't playing"—and shot at them, hitting one. The bullet remains lodged in the man's hip. The White man continued to yell racial slurs even when police shocked him with a stun gun and arrested him. (September 2014)

Local Resources

American Civil Liberties Union of Colorado: aclu-co.org, (303) 777-5482
Attorney General: coag.gov
Civil Rights Education and Enforcement Center: creeclaw.org
CO Civil Rights Division: colorado.gov/pacific/dora/civil-rights
CO NAACP: naacpstateconference.org; naacpdenver.org, (720) 210-9889

CONNECTICUT
11.6% Black
(about 415,000 out of 3,500,000)

	Black	White
Poverty Rate	n/a	6%
Unemployment Rate	n/a	3.5%
Imprisonment Ratio	9.4	1

Open carry permitted: YES	Stand your ground law: NO
Active hate groups: 2	2016 election result: Democrat

CONNECTICUT (cont.)

Percentage of Black victims of law enforcement killings (2013-16):
16%
(4 out of 25)

Notable Incidents

A video featuring a party at which some participants wore Ku Klux Klan outfits was circulated on social media. The region in question has some contemporary history with Klan-like gatherings. (November 2016)

A Quinnipiac University student posted a Snapchat picture of herself imitating blackface with a skincare mask and captioned the image "Black lives matter." (September 2016)

THOMAS LANE (37) was involved in a serious car crash. When Lane, who had suffered a head injury, behaved erratically and fought responders trying to free him from the mangled car, police used a stun gun on him. Lane's was the 18th stun gun-related death since 2005 in Connecticut, where two-thirds of the fatalities have been Black or Hispanic. (February 2016)

A White woman (Elaine Rothenberg) was reported as being armed and having accosted passersby. When confronted by police, the woman aimed the gun at them. She was not shot and was arrested unharmed. The weapon turned out to be a BB gun. (December 2015)

Fliers from the United Klans of America were distributed in neighborhoods. (July 2013)

Local Resources

American Civil Liberties Union of Connecticut: acluct.org, (860) 523-9146
Commission on Human Rights and Opportunities:
ct.gov/chro, (800) 477-5737
Connecticut NAACP: greaterhartfordnaacp.org, naacpnewhaven.org

---

DISTRICT OF COLUMBIA
48.3% Black
(about 329,000 out of 681,000)

	Black	White
Poverty Rate	28%	4%
Unemployment Rate	12.8%	2.4%
Imprisonment Ratio	8.2	1

Open carry permitted: NO	Stand your ground law: NO
Active hate groups: 2	2016 election result: Democrat

Percentage of Black victims of law enforcement killings (2013-16):
95.2%
(20 out of 21)

Notable Incidents

TERRENCE STERLING (31) was chased by police for reckless driving on a motorcycle. The chase was in violation of orders and department policy. An officer blocked his path with a police car, causing him to collide. When he attempted to flee, he was shot dead. (September 2016)

MIRIAM CAREY (34) rammed

her car into barricades near the White House before leading police on a chase. She was shot five times from behind with her 1-year-old child in the back seat. (October 2013)

Local Resources

ACLU of the District of Columbia: acludc.org, (202) 457-0800
Office of Human Rights: ohr.dc.gov, (202) 727-4559
Washington, DC NAACP: naacpdc.org, (202) 667-1700

DELAWARE
22.4% Black
(about 213,000 out of 950,000)

	Black	White
Poverty Rate	18%	8%
Unemployment Rate	7.8%	4.1%
Imprisonment Ratio	4.8	1

Open carry permitted: YES	Stand your ground law: NO
Active hate groups: 2	2016 election result: Democrat

Percentage of Black victims of law enforcement killings (2013-16):
36.4%
(4 out of 11)

Notable Incidents

A racist and anti-immigrant letter was distributed on car windshields around election time. The letter closed as follows: "In 2016 we need to vote American, we need to vote Christian, we need to vote white and we need to vote the

Obama regime out of office everyone [sic] of them." (November 2016)

A statement threatening African-American students at a high school was made through a text message. The student perpetrators were identified, and administrators stated that disciplinary action was to be taken. (November 2015)

> **I DON'T WANT THIS NEGRO STANDING NEXT TO ME.**
> —defendant refusing a Black lawyer

JEREMY MCDOLE (28) was a paraplegic who had been reported to police as having shot himself. Cell phone footage of the police response shows that McDole was quickly shot once for not putting his hands up and then shot several more times as he appears to adjust himself in his wheelchair. The attorney general declined to bring charges. (September 2015)

Hearings were held regarding racial allegations by Blacks employed in Delaware state government. Among other things, they noted the existence of a culture of discrimination, including race-based insults, lack of consideration for promotions, and punishment for reporting mistreatment. (July 2015)

In a recorded encounter with two White police officers, **Lateef Dickerson** complied with orders to get down on the ground and was kicked in the face as he did so. The kick knocked him unconscious and broke his jaw. A recording of the incident was only released after multiple ACLU lawsuits. A grand jury refused to indict. Subsequent charges for felony assault were filed, but a jury acquitted based on the officer's assertion that he had been aiming elsewhere. A separation agreement with the police department netted the officer $230,000. (August 2013)

Local Resources

American Civil Liberties Union of Delaware: aclu-de.org, (302) 654-3966
Delaware NAACP: newarkbranchnaacp.org, wilmingtondenaacp.org
State of Delaware Division of Human Relations:
statehumanrelations.delaware.gov

FLORIDA
16.8% Black
(about 3,500,000 out of 20,600,000)

	Black	White
Poverty Rate	24%	11%
Unemployment Rate	8.2%	4%
Imprisonment Ratio	3.6	1

Open carry permitted: NO	Stand your ground law: YES
Active hate groups: 26	2016 election result: Republican

Percentage of Black victims of law enforcement killings (2013-16):
35.3%
(131 out of 371)

Notable Incidents

Handwritten signs were posted labeling a pair of First Coast High School water fountains "colored" and "whites only." (November 2016)

Bathroom graffiti at Oviedo High School, which is predominately White, read: "Yall Black ppl better start picking yall slave numbers. KKK. 4Lyfe. GO TRUMP. 2016." A heart was drawn next to KKK. (November 2016)

The day after the 2016 presidential election, a White teacher at Wesley Chapel High School told Black students, "Don't make me call Donald Trump to get you sent back to Africa." (November 2016)

Fliers with messages from White supremacist group American Vanguard were found posted around the University of Central Florida campus. (November 2016)

A White male flying a large Confederate flag from the back of a pickup truck plastered with Trump stickers was arrested for two separate altercations with Black drivers during which he wielded a wrench and a baseball bat, respectively, and yelled racial slurs. (November 2016)

Students at Florida Gulf Coast University protested the school administration's response after a second incident of racist graffiti was found. The first read "KILL NIGGERS" and included a drawing of a stick figure hanging from a tree. The second read "Noose Tying 101." (November 2016)

A White homeowner in Kendall, FL created a lynching scene in his front yard using two dark-looking figures. Upon receiving complaints and accusations of racism, he added a sign reading "PLEASE DON'T BE IGNORANT IT'S HALLOWEEN." (October 2016)

A White man was a passenger in a car when he engaged in an argument with the Black male driver and White woman passenger in another vehicle, at one point shouting "nigger lover." There were four children with the interracial couple. Moments later, he tossed a can of beer at the couple's car and then pointed a handgun at them. The man was arrested. (September 2016)

A young autism patient under the care of **Charles Kinsey** had slipped away from a group home. North Miami police responded based on a call of a man with a gun. Cell phone video showed an unarmed Kinsey and his patient, who was holding a toy truck, being held at gunpoint by police. Though the patient did not respond to the police, Kinsey complied with all demands by lying on the ground with his hands in the air. An officer shot Kinsey in the leg. (July 2016)

Three West Port High School students bullied classmates by waving Confederate flags during school. (January 2016)

COREY JONES (31) was heading home when his car broke down around 3am. As he spoke to a roadside assistance operator on the phone, a plainclothes officer in an unmarked police van pulled over erratically, and the officer who got out immediately treated Jones—a lawful concealed carry permit holder with a gun in an open carry state—as a criminal. Recorded audio from the roadside assistance call was as follows:

– Officer: "You good?"
– Jones: "I'm good."
– Officer (sarcastic, forceful): "Really?"
– Jones: "Yeah."
– Officer: "Get your fuckin' hands up! Get your fuckin' hands up!"
– Jones (starting to run): "Hold on! Hold on, man!"

Seconds later, Jones had been shot six times. The officer subsequently lied about all aspects of the exchange, portraying Jones as the aggressor. He was indicted for the murder. (October 2015)

Retired Army sergeant **Wayne Scott** was out of town when someone spray painted the following message on his home: "DUMB NIGGER BLACK

LIVES MATTER FOR TARGET PRACTICE." (September 2015)

Two ranking Miami Beach police officers are no longer with the department after the discovery of racist e-mails. The messages included hundreds of racist jokes and memes, including a photo of a baby in a KFC bucket purporting to put to rest questions about Barack Obama's place of birth and a meme of a "Black Monopoly" board game for which every square is labeled "go to jail." The investigation mandated a bias review of cases against minorities that had relied on the officers' testimony. (May 2015)

Three current and former employees of the Florida Department of Corrections were also members of the Traditionalist American Knights of the Ku Klux Klan. An FBI informant recorded all three men making plans to murder a former inmate, who is Black. In the recordings, the men often referred to the inmate using a racial epithet. They were arrested for conspiracy. (April 2015)

A group of about 100 students marched from Florida State University to the Capitol to protest racism in Florida's prison system. The rally, organized by the Students for a Democratic Society at FSU, was prompted by the distribution of recruitment flyers from the Ku Klux Klan in Tallahassee neighborhoods and reports of racist attacks on prisoners by the Department of Corrections. Some noted violent or suspicious deaths of Black prisoners in Florida include:

- **DARREN RAINEY** (50), a schizophrenic man who had defecated on himself and was locked into a shower stall with external temperature controls for two hours; he was found deceased with second- and third-degree burns. His death was ruled an accident.

- **JERRY WASHINGTON** (54), who had filed complaints against corrections officers who warned they would retaliate on "pick-a-nigga Friday"; Washington and fellow inmates alleged a climate of racism, brutality, negligence, and sexual harassment at the prison.
- **MATTHEW WALKER** (46), who, while handcuffed, was beaten and stomped so badly by as many as 18 correctional officers that his larynx was crushed and his throat was swollen shut; his death was one of several prisoner fatalities that caused major scandal for the Florida Department of Corrections, leading to the firing of 32 guards.
- **LATANDRA ELLINGTON** (36), who, after reporting officer misconduct with another female prisoner, was found dead in a confinement cell. (April 2015)

Fliers from the Traditionalist American Knights of the Ku Klux Klan were left in driveways. (March 2015)

> Shut that nigger baby up.
> —flight passenger

After an internal investigation uncovered the exchange of blatantly racist text messages, which included talk of "killing niggers" and having "the noose ready" and a cobbled together video of racist images, four officers are no longer employed by the Fort Lauderdale Police Department. The officers had worked in a predominantly Black neighborhood. (March 2015)

ANDREW ANTHONY WILLIAMS (48) was the eleventh victim that night of a police "reverse sting," a tactic that targets street-level drug buyers and inserts them into the criminal justice system. When Williams tried to escape by car, he was gunned down. (March 2015)

A White male fellow bar patron told **Kenneth Hodge** "this bar is not for blacks." After Hodge ignored him, the man hit him on the head with a beer bottle. (February 2015)

A Saturday trip to a shooting range for **Sergeant Valerie Deant** and other soldiers, who were there for an annual weapons qualification training, led to a shocking discovery. The North Miami Beach Police had used the range before them for a training and had left behind their targets: actual mug shots of exclusively Black men. When the police chief was questioned about the practice, he indicated that it violated no policies and that no discipline was in order. (January 2015)

On a trip to Walmart, 62-year-old **Clarence Daniels** was lawfully carrying a firearm when a White man tackled him to the ground and two other White men joined in holding him down and taking his gun, despite his explanations that he was a licensed gun owner with a concealed carry permit. The man who attacked him was later arrested for assault. (January 2015)

A White man was charged with abuse after he poked a 10-year-old Black boy in the chest and forehead, telling him, "you are a nigger—wash your dirty skin." He also told the child that his own skin was better because it was white. When interviewed, the man admitted to using the slur and to being racist. "I was taught growing up that you don't associate with them," he said. He also blamed the country's crime problems on people of color and said he would never have moved into his home had he known many of his neighbors were African American. (July 2014)

A White male criminal defendant refused the assistance of a Black public defender, stating "I don't want this negro standing next to me." (July 2014)

Fliers from the Loyal White Knights of the Ku Klux Klan were left at residences in a neighborhood. (March 2014)

The NFL concluded an investigation against a White Miami Dolphins player who once called fellow Dolphin **Jonathan Martin** a "half-nigger piece of shit" on a voicemail and joked about the usefulness of a rifle for "shooting black people." The player was found responsible for a pattern of racist and homophobic harassment. (February 2014)

In November 2012, **JORDAN DAVIS** (17) and his friends were asked by a White man to turn down the music they were playing in their vehicle in a convenience store parking lot. After words were exchanged, the man, who was quoted as saying "you are not going to talk to me like that," retrieved a gun from his car and fired ten rounds at Davis's vehicle, killing him. The man was imprisoned for the shooting, and letters he sent from prison were released by the state's attorney in 2014. Passages included:

- "This jail is full of blacks and they all act like thugs. ... This may sound a bit radical but if more people would arm themselves and kill these **** idiots when they're threatening you, eventually they may take the hint and change their behavior."
- "The more time I am exposed to these people, the more prejudiced against them I become."

(February 2014)

Ku Klux Klan fliers were distributed in neighborhoods that were predominantly Black and Latino. (November 2013)

WHAT DO APPLES AND BLACK PEOPLE HAVE IN COMMON?

❦

They Both Hang From Trees.

—sheriff's deputy

An officer stopped **Dontrell Stephens**, who was on a bicycle, to ticket him for a traffic infraction. Within seconds, the officer shot Stephens four times, one of which entered his inner bicep, indicating that his hands were raised, as he claimed they had been. Another bullet entered his back, as he tried to flee, piercing his spinal cord and paralyzing him from the waist down. The officer claimed he thought Stephens had a gun; Stephens was actually holding a flip phone. (September 2013)

JERMAINE MCBEAN (33) had just purchased a BB rifle from a pawn shop and was walking home with it. He was perceived as a threat by police officers and killed. Florida is an explicitly open carry state. (July 2013)

In a classroom with about 40 other students, a Hispanic male student at Full Sail University walked up behind **Tavoris Murray**, told him he hated Black people, and stabbed him with a screwdriver. When deputies arrived, the man said, among other things, that "African Americans do nothing but steal." (February 2013)

Local Resources

American Civil Liberties Union of Florida: aclufl.org, (786) 363-2700
Florida Commission on Human Relations: http: fchr.state.fl.us
Florida NAACP: flnaacp.com, (407) 843-5320

GEORGIA
31.7% Black
(about 3,300,000 out of 10,300,000)

	Black	White
Poverty Rate	31%	9%
Unemployment Rate	8.9%	3.5%
Imprisonment Ratio	3.2	1

Open carry permitted: YES	Stand your ground law: YES
Active hate groups: 15	2016 election result: Republican

Percentage of Black victims of law enforcement killings (2013-16):
42.4% (56 out of 132)

Notable Incidents

Collins Hill High School was heavily defaced with hate-filled graffiti that included slurs directed toward Blacks, gays, and Hispanics as well as swastikas and the word "Trump." (November 2016)

> RUN, NIGGER, RUN!
> —judge

Two White male officers once part of an all-White traffic unit that aggressively patrolled I-95 in South Georgia were removed from the force after an internal affairs investigation uncovered racist messages exchanged over Facebook. The two officers sent derogatory jokes that referred to African Americans as "colored people" and "niggers." They also made direct reference to the targeting of Black motorists:

– "It's supposed to rain tomorrow. Might not get too

many niggs."
– "I hope we get a few but [expletive] if we don't." (October 2016)

A Georgia teacher's aide was fired after racist posts were found on her Facebook page, including comments labeling Michelle Obama a "gorilla." (October 2016)

A White Georgia resident had experienced the chairman of the Douglas County Board of Commissioners making racial comments in the past, so when he had the chance to speak with him again, he recorded it. The man suggested that if the Black candidate for sheriff won, he would "put a bunch of blacks in leadership positions," that they would be unqualified, and that Black officials would cause bankruptcy. (October 2016)

A White man posted a photo of himself in his office with his co-worker's 3-year-old child, **Cayden Jenkins**. His Facebook friends responded by calling the child names like "Toby" and "Sambo" and asking when he had become a slave owner. Instead of admonishing his friends, he joined in on the mocking, calling the child "feral." He was fired. (October 2016)

A home in Lawrenceville was defaced with the words "NIGGER" and the letters "KKK." (October 2016)

Construction worker **Nelson King** was working on a road when a White man pulled up and began saying things like "Get these niggers off the road; I live here" and "I'll kill you, nigger." When the man pointed a gun at him, King began recording the incident with his cellphone. The man was arrested on multiple charges. (September 2016)

When a White man (Bryant Brough) was pulled over by

police, he immediately brandished a firearm. He was not shot. An officer stated of the police involved: "This was clearly a situation that could have escalated into a lethal force, [but] through their skillful verbal commands and de-escalation tools, they were able to get the guy to surrender." (July 2016)

DERAVIS CAINE ROGERS (22) was driving out of his apartment building parking lot when a White police officer, seeking a suspect who had been breaking into cars, shot him as he passed. The director of the Racial Justice Action Center subsequently called on Atlanta's police chief "to acknowledge that killings happen when officers are trained to see community members as enemies and neighborhoods as combat zones to occupy. Until we get rid of broken window policing and policing for profit, we will continue to see officers violating the rights of—and sometimes ending the lives of—our friends, neighbors, and fellow residents." The officer who shot Rogers was fired and subsequently indicted for murder, making him the second Georgia officer in more than five years to be indicted for the killing of a civilian. (June 2016)

A far-right Confederate rally was held at Stone Mountain to commemorate Confederate Memorial Day. At the same time in Rome, GA, the Ku Klux Klan—in full regalia— together with the neo-Nazi National Socialist Movement and the Aryan Nation, conducted a "free speech" rally in front of the Floyd County Law Enforcement Center. (April 2016)

When White policemen approached **Patrick Mumford** sitting in a parked car in a driveway with friends, he was not the target of their warrant.

Despite him providing his name, which was not the name of the target, the officers told him that he was the target, never asked for identification, refused his requests to see the warrant, tased him, and arrested him. Body cameras recorded the encounter. (February 2016)

A Georgia state representative introducing a bill to protect Confederate monuments spoke in defense of the Ku Klux Klan, saying it "was not so much a racist thing but a vigilante thing to keep law and order" and "it made a lot of people straighten up." (January 2016)

A White male firefighter was in an Applebee's restaurant making racial comments to his wife about a waitress. **Marquist Curtis**, seated nearby, verbally confronted the man, and a fight ensued. Curtis and his wife left the restaurant, but the firefighter followed, retrieved a handgun from his vehicle, and pointed it at the couple. In addition to losing his job, the firefighter was charged with, among other things, aggravated assault, battery (for kicking Curtis in the chest), and unbecoming language (for continued and repeated use of the N-word during the incident). (October 2015)

After a Black student at Georgia Institute of Technology said three Phi Delta Theta members had shouted racial slurs at her from the windows of the fraternity house, more than 100 students protested outside the house. Some of the demonstrators covered their mouths with duct tape with racial slurs printed on it. (August 2015)

For two days, a group of Confederate flag supporters called "Respect the Flag" rode around in the Atlanta suburbs terrorizing and threatening

Black families while using racial slurs and pointing firearms. The group targeted a Black child's birthday party, where members threatened to kill partygoers. A White couple that loaded a gun and confronted the family with it was arrested, convicted, and sentenced to 15 years in prison. (July 2015)

ANTHONY HILL (27) ran unarmed and completely naked toward a police officer. The officer shot him twice. (March 2015)

When **Tiambrya Jenkins** and a White female student got into a fight, both girls were transferred to an alternative high school. The White student was allowed to return after 90 days; Jenkins had to stay in the alternative school for a year. (September 2014)

Ku Klux Klan fliers were left on cars in Atlanta. (July 2014)

When 69-year-old **Dhoruba Bin-Wahad** tried to move into his new home, he was reported as a burglar. Police arrived, and a White officer effected a forceful arrest on the man, slamming his head against a concrete porch in the process. The officer claimed Bin-Wahad had been combative, but cell phone video from a bystander proved this false. The officer was indicted for assault. (May 2014)

ZIKARIOUS FLINT (20) was reported for having a gun. He was chased by police and shot twice in the back. Open carrying of a gun in Georgia is expressly permitted by law. (March 2014)

About 50 people attended a rally held by the neo-Confederate hate group the League of the South. (August 2013)

Wilcox County High School,

three hours south of Atlanta, has for decades had its prom—an explicitly Whites-only event—funded and organized by parents rather than the school. In 2013, a mixed-race group of students attempted to organize an integrated prom. Their attempt was met with resistance, and the Whites-only event was still held. (April 2013)

Recruiting fliers from the Loyal White Knights of the Ku Klux Klan were left in the driveways of residences. (January 2013)

Local Resources

American Civil Liberties Union of Georgia: acluga.org, (770) 303-8111
Georgia NAACP: naacpga.org, (404) 577-8977

HAWAII
2.6% Black
(about 37,000 out of 1,400,000)

	Black	White
Poverty Rate	n/a	7%
Unemployment Rate	n/a	3.9%
Imprisonment Ratio	2.4	1

Open carry permitted: YES	Stand your ground law: NO
Active hate groups: 0	2016 election result: Democrat

Percentage of Black victims of law enforcement killings (2013-16):
5%
(1 out of 20)

Local Resources

American Civil Liberties Union of Hawaii: acluhi.org, (808) 522-5900
Hawaii Civil Rights Commission: labor.hawaii.gov/hcrc, (808) 586-8636
Hawaii NAACP: naacphawaii.zohosites.com

IDAHO
0.8% Black
(about 13,000 out of 1,600,000)

	Black	White
Poverty Rate	n/a	11%
Unemployment Rate	n/a	3.7%
Imprisonment Ratio	4.7	1

Open carry permitted: YES	Stand your ground law: NO
Active hate groups: 3	2016 election result: Republican

Percentage of Black victims of law enforcement killings (2013-16):
0%
(0 out of 22)

Notable Incidents

An intoxicated White male (Avery Tusch) battered police officers attempting to take him into custody, at one point securing an officer in a chokehold. Tusch was not shot. (July 2016)

Ku Klux Klan fliers were left in driveways throughout a neighborhood. (March 2015)

FUCK YOUR BREATH.
—police officer

Fliers from the Traditionalist American Knights were distributed. (January 2015)

A 60-year-old White male Idaho resident on a flight was seated next to a White woman with her 19-month-old biracial son on her lap. As the plane descended, the child started crying. The man told the woman to "shut that nigger baby up." When she asked what he said, he leaned in with his face next to hers, repeated the statement, and then slapped the child's face, leaving a scratch below the baby's right eye. He was arrested for assault and pleaded guilty in court. (February 2013)

Local Resources

American Civil Liberties Union of Idaho: acluidaho.org, (208) 344-9750
Idaho Commission on Human Rights: humanrights.idaho.gov, (208) 334-2873
Idaho NAACP: naacptristateinu.org, (801) 250-5088

ILLINOIS
14.7% Black
(about 1,900,000 out of 12,800,000)

	Black	White
Poverty Rate	23%	7%
Unemployment Rate	13.1%	4.2%
Imprisonment Ratio	8.8	1

Open carry permitted: NO	Stand your ground law: NO
Active hate groups: 13	2016 election result: Democrat

ILLINOIS (cont.)

Percentage of Black victims of law enforcement killings (2013-16):
52.8%
(65 out of 123)

Notable Incidents

After the election, a student at Southern Illinois University at Carbondale posted a photo to social media of two people in blackface in front of a Confederate flag. The university confirmed that the woman in the photo is a student but said that the man is not. (November 2016)

After the shooting of **Joshua Beal**, Black Lives Matter activists in a mostly White neighborhood encountered a group of angry White people with a Blue Lives Matter flag. In a video posted by the activists, a man said if you don't support police, you're a criminal. The police took a baseball bat from one member of the group. One of the activists described the scene:

"White people are driving by and yelling at us 'Nigger go home! Get the fuck out of here! Blue Lives Matter!' More of them got out of the car and chanted 'CPD! Blue Lives Matter.'" The activists had to be escorted to their cars. (November 2016)

The following text exchange between Marist High School students around the time of the Joshua Beal shooting was later shared on Twitter:
– "I FUCKING HATE NIGGERS"
– "same"
(November 2016)

A White female Donald Trump delegate from Chicago was stripped of her credentials after she put this caption on a

Facebook photo of law enforcement officials on the roof at the Republican National Convention's welcome party: "Our brave snipers just waiting for some n------ to try something. Love them." Her social media handle was "whitepride." (July 2016)

At a festival in Chicago, **Ernest Crim III** and his wife wanted to play a bean bag toss game, but the group at the next station had all the bags. After he retrieved a stray one from the field, a White woman in the other group called him a nigger. When he began recording her, she first knocked the phone out of his hands and then called him a nigger repeatedly. When he asked her name, she spat on his wife. The woman was later arrested for a hate crime. (July 2016)

A biracial teenager was with friends at a campground lake near Canton, IL. A pair of White males began beating up the teenager and yelling racist epithets. Their mother, who was on hand, encouraged the attack, yelling "Kill that nigger!" Midway through the beating, the teenager ended up back in the water, where the attackers reportedly began holding his head under the surface. A bystander recorded the attack on cell phone video. The attackers and their mother were arrested. (June 2016)

After a Black student at Southern Illinois University complained that student Trump supporters used a racial slur and said Black students should "go back to Africa" at a Carbondale campus residence hall forum, a video entitled "SIUC White is Right" was posted to YouTube. The video ended with this Anonymous-style call to action in a computer-generated voice:

> "...we send out this broadcast in hopes of reaching out to all the hard-working White

Americans out there. We will not stand for these niggers any longer. I want us all on May 2 to band together and beat us up some niggers, too. ...don't forget your baseball bats. I want to see the trees riddled with as much black fruit as they can hold. Hitler did nothing wrong, and neither will we. White power."
(April 2016)

Black parents of students at Kenwood Academy on the South Side of Chicago complained about a skit performed by suburban Barrington High School during the Illinois Junior Classical Convention. The skit involved White students humorously depicting a slave auction. (February 2016)

Northwestern University PhD student **Lawrence Crosby** stopped to fix an issue with his driver's side door before driving away. A White woman called the police, accusing him of stealing the car. On being signaled by police, dashcam footage shows that Crosby pulled over, stepped out of the car with his hands in the air, and was tackled by five officers who kneed and punched him during the takedown. Even after determining that the car was his, Crosby was arrested and charged with disobeying officers and resisting arrest. A civil lawsuit is pending. (October 2015)

A silent protest at Illinois Wesleyan University was staged in response to the N-word being found written on a campus sidewalk and an environment of "microaggressions" in classes (e.g., comments being made that are offensive or make students feel singled out or uncomfortable). (September 2015)

Both Black and White University of Illinois women's basketball team players corroborated allegations that Black players on the predominantly White team were treated differently. The Black girls were put on a separate squad dubbed "the dog pound," were segregated from other players in hotels at away games, and were insulted with attacks on their race and character, including statements that their "culture" was "toxic" and "poison" to the rest of the team. The treatment was so bad that four players transferred to other schools. (July 2015)

Swastikas and "disparaging remarks about African Americans" were among the graffiti found on four separate occasions at Northwestern University, causing the school to launch a hate crime investigation. (June 2015)

Oakwood High School was forced to increase security after a White student's tweet about protestors in Ferguson, MO: "I don't feel sorry for black people. If you hate us so much GO BACH [sic] TO AFRICA. We should have never bought you. I mean this wouldn't happen if black people wouldn't act like hooligans. We don't start a riot when white ppl die." (November 2014)

In the middle of a grocery store with other shoppers around, a White man pulled out a knife and stabbed a 79-year-old Black woman four times. The man, who had a history of animosity toward African Americans, later stated that her being elderly and Black made her an "easy target." (October 2014)

LAQUAN MCDONALD (17) came to police attention for allegedly attempting to break into cars and for being armed with a small knife. In an initial encounter, McDonald, who had PCP in his system, punctured a police car tire with his knife.

In the next encounter, police cars pulled up toward McDonald, who was walking down the middle of the street. He had a knife in his hand and, as he moved away from the officers, one of them shot him once, which dropped him to the ground. The officer then continued to shoot him, ultimately emptying his full clip of 16 bullets into the boy. Police initially reported that McDonald had lunged at them with the knife, but dashcam footage proved this to be a lie. Several officers were charged with obstruction of justice and misconduct, and the shooter was charged with murder. The case was also the impetus for a U.S. Department of Justice investigation into the Chicago Police Department. (October 2014)

A White man was angered that **Judge Arnette Hubbard**, who was 79 at the time, was smoking a cigarette so close to him. After a verbal exchange between them, he said, "Rosa Parks, move!" before spitting in her face. Hubbard grabbed him as he tried to leave, and he turned around and slapped her across the face. At trial, a White judge acquitted the man, suggesting that Hubbard had initiated the incident and that both parties should have been able to settle their differences more maturely. (July 2014)

> **ALL LIVES MATTER.**
>
> **And if you think it's just black lives kiss my ass bitch and go back to the fields that us in the north fought to free you from.**
>
> **—F I R E M A N**

Fliers from the Loyal White Knights of the Ku Klux Klan were distributed in a neighborhood. (July 2014)

MICHAEL TINGLING (59) had stepped in front of his 15-year-old daughter after a White man made an inappropriate gesture toward the girl. The White man said, "What, nigger?" before punching Tingling in the chest twice during a brief confrontation. Moments later, Tingling, who wore a pacemaker, was rushed to a hospital in full cardiac arrest. The White man was ultimately charged with murder and a hate crime. (March 2014)

Fliers from the Traditionalist American Knights were left at residences in a neighborhood. (December 2013)

Dashcam footage showed a Chicago police officer holding his gun sideways and emptying its full clip into a stolen car with six Black teens inside. The car was reversing away from him at the time, and he continued firing even after it struck a pole. Two of the teens were hit, and the officer faced federal charges for the incident. (December 2013)

A White man pleaded guilty to a hate crime after a confrontation with two Black men, one of whom was his new neighbor. During the confrontation, he used a racial slur, spat in the face of one of the men, and brandished a knife. He later threw a rock through a glass door of the man's apartment and slashed a tire on one of the men's vehicles. (October 2013)

Local Resources

American Civil Liberties Union of Illinois: aclu-mo.org, (312) 201-9740
Illinois Human Rights Commission: illinois.gov/ihrc
Illinois NAACP: illinoisnaacp.org

INDIANA
9.6% Black
(about 637,000 out of 6,600,000)

	Black	White
Poverty Rate	28%	12%
Unemployment Rate	n/a	3.8%
Imprisonment Ratio	4.8	1

Open carry permitted: NO	Stand your ground law: YES
Active hate groups: 21	2016 election result: Republican

Percentage of Black victims of law enforcement killings (2013-16):
32.9%
(25 out of 76)

Notable Incidents

A Black church was marked "kill all koons" and "koons inside." (December 2016)

The N-word was painted on the side of a Black family's home. Prior to this, they had received harassing notes that included the phrases "white power" and "Trump country" and that directed them to "Go back where you came from. You are not wanted around here." (December 2016)

A swastika and the letters "KKK" were found spray-painted on Bloomington's B-Line Trail. (November 2016)

Black students at DePauw University found the nameplates ripped off their doors and the inscription "H8 Niggers" written on a message board. (September 2016)

Fliers from the Traditionalist American Knights of the Ku

Klux Klan were left in yards. (October 2014)

During a vehicle stop for seat belt violation, the female driver produced her information, and then officers requested ID from passenger **Jamal Jones.** He informed them that he didn't have an ID but sought instead to produce a recent traffic violation with his information, which prompted officers to draw guns. He offered them the document, but they insisted he step out of the vehicle. He asked for a supervisor. Officers then smashed the car window and tased him. Two children were in the back seat, one of whom recorded the incident via cell phone. (September 2014)

Ku Klux Klan fliers were distributed to homes and businesses. (July 2013)

Local Resources

American Civil Liberties Union of Indiana: aclu-in.org, (317) 635-4059
Indiana Civil Rights Commission: in.gov/icrc, (317) 232-2600
Indiana NAACP: indianascnaacp.org; indynaacp.org; naacpgary.org

IOWA
3.5% Black
(about 109,000 out of 3,100,000)

	Black	White
Poverty Rate	n/a	9%
Unemployment Rate	n/a	2.8%
Imprisonment Ratio	11.1	1

Open carry permitted: YES	Stand your ground law: NO
Active hate groups: 3	2016 election result: Republican

IOWA (cont.)

Percentage of Black victims of law enforcement killings (2013-16):
11.5%
(3 out of 26)

Notable Incidents

A White man (Scott Michael Greene) engaged in racial harassment of Blacks, including use of the N-word and Confederate flags. After an arrest and court appearance, the man retaliated against police, who he claimed had violated his constitutional rights, by ambushing and killing two officers. (November 2016)

McKinley Elementary School was defaced by graffiti that included the N-word, "KKK," and "Trump." (November 2016)

Racist signs were posted throughout the campus of Iowa State University. Messages included: "In 1950 America was 90% white. It is now only 50% white. Will you become a minority in your own country?" Two weeks prior, similar signs had been posted at the University of Iowa, including one that read "Are you sick of anti-White propaganda in college? YOU ARE NOT ALONE." (October 2016)

When Iowa newspaper *The Gazette* posted a story about three White male college students arrested for burglary, they published it with yearbook photos of the men. When they published a story about four Black men arrested for burglary the very next day, they used mugshots. (March 2015)

In Council Bluffs, the detached garage of a White woman with a biracial daughter was vandalized with the N-word, a Nazi swastika, and the letters WP. About two days later, the garage was set on fire. (January 2015)

Local Resources

American Civil Liberties Union of Iowa: aclu-ia.org, (515) 243-3988
Iowa Civil Rights Commission: icrc.iowa.gov, (515) 281-4121
Iowa NAACP: iowanebraskanaacp.org; naacpdesmoines.com

KANSAS
6.3% Black
(about 183,000 out of 2,900,000)

	Black	White
Poverty Rate	27%	11%
Unemployment Rate	n/a	3.7%
Imprisonment Ratio	7	1

Open carry permitted: YES	Stand your ground law: YES
Active hate groups: 4	2016 election result: Republican

Percentage of Black victims of law enforcement killings (2013-16):
19.1%
(9 out of 47)

Notable Incidents

Kansas City's main library was defaced with racist graffiti. (December 2016)

A high school student's drawing of a KKK hood with the words "kill all blacks" was posted to Snapchat. The school stated that disciplinary measures would be taken. (December 2016)

A White female Kansas University cheerleader posted a Snapchat of three White male students standing side-by-side in "K" sweaters with the caption "KKK go trump." All four students were suspended. (November 2016)

A small liberal arts college in Lindsborg, KS was the target of racist graffiti written on its walkways in chalk. Messages included "Make Lindsborg White Again" and a chalk outline of a dead body. The culprit later called the president of the college, who has two adopted biracial children, to tell him that the messaging was targeted at him. The caller also asserted that he and the other perpetrators were members of the California-based White Nationalist group Identity Evropa. (September 2016)

A White female Kansas State University student posted a Snapchat of her and another White female with charcoal skincare masks on their faces, their fingers in a mock gang sign, and the caption "Feels good to finally be a nigga." (September 2016)

A Wichita woman with six biracial grandchildren received a handwritten letter by mail that read as follows:
> My wife and I have lived in this area for many a year. We have noticed that there are some black children at your residence. Maybe you are running a daycare or these are your children. In either case, we have put our house for sale. This neighborhood does not need any blacks in it. There is a reason for the saying, "The other side of the tracks." That is where these people belong. You have done a great disrespect in this

neighborhood by not thinking of your neighbors. (August 2016)

> BLACK MAN: YOU GOT A LIGHT?
> —
> WHITE WOMAN:
> I HAVE NEVER BEEN SO AFRAID OF ANYTHING IN MY WHOLE LIFE, I DON'T THINK.

After the Dallas police officer shootings, **LaNaydra Williams** received a comment from a White male Kansas police officer on a Facebook photo of her daughter. It read: "We'll see how much her life matters soon.. better be careful leaving your info open where she can be found :) hold her close tonight, it'll be the last time." Williams reported the threat, and the officer was fired that same day. (June 2016)

CRAIG MCKINNIS (44) was being subjected to a traffic stop when it was discovered that he had a criminal warrant. McKinnis allegedly resisted arrest and tried to flee. Officers placed him in a chokehold and ignored multiple complaints of "I can't breathe." The restraint was released when he became unresponsive. He later died at the hospital. (May 2014)

Local Resources

American Civil Liberties Union of Kansas: aclu-kansas.org
Kansas Human Rights Commission: khrc.net, (785) 296-3206
Kansas NAACP: http: kansasnaacp.blogspot.com

KENTUCKY
8.3% Black
(about 368,000 out of 4,400,000)

	Black	White
Poverty Rate	36%	17%
Unemployment Rate	n/a	4.4%
Imprisonment Ratio	3.3	1

Open carry permitted: YES	Stand your ground law: YES
Active hate groups: 16	2016 election result: Republican

Percentage of Black victims of law enforcement killings (2013-16):
16.2%
(11 out of 68)

Notable Incidents

A group text message between football players at a high school showed one White player issuing the threat "I'm gonna lynch you" to Black freshman teammate **DaMarco Vinegar**. Other race-based language included suggesting that Vinegar should pick cotton and sell crack and that he didn't know who his father was. Harassment charges were filed. (April 2016)

A Black student from the University of Louisville was shoved and verbally abused during a protest at a Trump rally. **Shiya Nwanguma** reported that she "was called a nigger and a cunt and got kicked out." (March 2016)

African-American students at the University of Kentucky held a town hall meeting to discuss the negative racial climate at the school. Issues included public hate speech, micro-aggressive behavior toward Blacks, and advisors steering Black students away from STEM careers. The meeting was initially prompted by the administration's failure to provide redress regarding an audio recording of White students making hateful and racist remarks about a Black classmate. (March 2016)

After **Judge Olu Stevens** revoked a White detainee's bond on drug charges, the man shouted "punk ass nigger" on his way out of the courtroom. The judge recalled him, held him in contempt, and sentenced him to an extra 60 days in jail. (January 2016)

White members of a fire department provided roadside assistance and transportation to a White man who had been involved in a traffic accident while ignoring **Chege**
Mwangi's family, which was the other party involved. In response to what should happen with the Black family, the fire department's chief was caught on body camera audio stating "We ain't taking no niggers here," followed by laughter. (November 2014)

Fliers from the Traditionalist American Knights of the Ku Klux Klan were distributed in a neighborhood. (July 2014)

A grand jury exonerated cousins **Tyrone Booker, Shaquazz Allen, Jerron Bush**, and **Craig Dean** on charges that they robbed a White woman at gunpoint. Allen and Booker also were cleared on separate charges filed when the victims of a different crime that same evening saw mug shots of the four young men on a local newscast about the robbery and then misidentified them as their assailants as well. The young men, some of whom spent up to 70 days locked up, were cleared in part by cellphone records showing that they could not have been at the crime scene. The "Misidentified 4," who blamed racial profiling for the incident, collected a large settlement from the police department and an apology from the mayor but stated that it did not remedy their distrust of local police, who breached policy by not separating the victim and a witness during the identification process. (March 2014)

Local Resources

American Civil Liberties Union of Kentucky: aclu-ky.org, (502) 581-1181
KY Commission on Human Rights: http: kchr.ky.gov, (502) 595-4024
Kentucky NAACP: kynaacp.org

LOUISIANA
32.5% Black
(about 1,500,000 out of 4,600,000)

	Black	White
Poverty Rate	31%	12%
Unemployment Rate	10.7%	4.1%
Imprisonment Ratio	4	1

Open carry permitted: YES	Stand your ground law: YES
Active hate groups: 7	2016 election result: Republican

Percentage of Black victims of law enforcement killings (2013-16):
50.5%
(47 out of 93)

Notable Incidents

A White man who shot and killed former NFL player **Joe McKnight** in an alleged road rage incident in Jefferson Parish was released with no charges that same day. In a press conference, the sheriff berated the Black community at length for its angered response. (December 2016)

When 8-year-old **Jordan Jackson** tried to defend his 4-year-old sister from a group of White children, one of whom was 13, he was told, "You need to go back to the cotton farm." Jordan suffered a broken arm and a concussion in the subsequent skirmish. (November 2016)

An Asian male Louisiana Tech student sent a Snapchat of himself with the caption "Got some triggered ass niggers in history class lmaoooo one said fight me and all I can think of is leaving her half dead." (November 2016)

The sheriff of Iberia Parish, who is White, was cleared of civil rights violation charges despite extensive testimony from former detectives on the department's authorized culture of racism and abuse. One detective testified that, after three drunken off-duty officers had beaten up two young Black men for fun, the sheriff chalked it up to a simple case of "nigger knockin'." Another testified that a supervisor pointed to a red stain on the floor next to a suspect who was being questioned and said, "That's from the last nigger I shot." Ten former deputies pleaded guilty to civil rights violations. (November 2016)

ALTON STERLING (37) was selling CDs in front of a gas station when he was reported for pointing a gun at someone. Upon arrival, two highly aggressive White officers wrestled him to the ground, then one yelled, "he's got a gun!" The officers shot him six times, after which one removed the gun from Sterling's pocket. No charges were filed against the officers. A wrongful death action from the family asserts that the "City of Baton Rouge has a long standing pervasive policy of tolerating racist behavior by some of its officers. There have also been multiple verbal racist comments by officers reported to the department. This tolerance of such behavior directly leads to the mistreatment of individuals of African-American descent." The suit cites two documented instances in which Baton Rouge police officers sent racist text messages to colleagues, including a reference to Black people protesting Sterling's death as "chimp[ing] out." (July 2016)

Although photos of Alton Sterling were readily available from Facebook and his family, CNN sought and used an old mugshot as the only photograph of Sterling to air for a report on the incident. Several media outlets, including CNN, have been called out repeatedly for using mugshots of Black victims of officer-involved shootings. (July 2016)

Police in Welsh, LA responded to a domestic disturbance at a White man's home. When officers gained entry, the man pointed a shotgun at them. He was not shot. (July 2016)

The Patriotic Brigade Knights of the Ku Klux Klan distributed fliers in a Louisiana parish. The fliers read: "You can sleep tonight knowing the Klan is awake!" (July 2016)

An employee at a restaurant in New Orleans's French Quarter included the text "NIGGER 100% DISLIKE" on **Gaynielle Neville**'s receipt. The employee was fired as a result of the incident. (May 2016)

KKK recruitment fliers from The Loyal White Knights were distributed in driveways on MLK Day. (January 2016)

After 17-year-old **Lyle Dotson** got separated from his French Quarter tour group of Ball State University students and faculty, which was in town on an architecture field trip, he was approached by three state troopers. They did not announce that they were members of law enforcement and grabbed Dotson's hands while ordering the teen, who was talking on the phone, to identify with whom he was speaking. The officers refused to offer a reason for Dotson's being detained or to give him their names or badge numbers. Dotson was also pushed against a building and searched without being told he had the right to refuse the search. The incident was included in a 2016 federal lawsuit against Louisiana State Police alleging a pattern of "deliberate indifference" to unconstitutional and racially biased arrests and citing several specific instances. (October 2015)

Despite every element of the dispatch not matching—the color of the truck, license plate, number of occupants, color of clothes, and location—two White state troopers "harshly interrogated, physically assaulted, knocked to the ground," tased several times, falsely arrested, and unjustly imprisoned **Michael Baugh** as he asserted that the officers were interrogating the wrong man. (September 2015)

A 12-year-old Black boy had gone into the gas station to pay for his grandmother's gas when a 54-year-old White man accosted him. Referencing the boy's long dreadlocks, the man asked if he was a girl. Surveillance video shows that he backed the boy into a shelf, hit him on the back of the head, and pulled his pants down several inches while calling him "nigger" and making other racially charged remarks. He was arrested and charged with a hate crime. (July 2015)

Art chosen for the annual Pontchatoula Strawberry Festival's poster was a depiction of two Black children in a pickaninny style with coal-black faces and bright red lips. After a resulting uproar, it was agreed that the posters would not be used. (April 2015)

A White Baton Rouge cop who worked in a Black community for fifteen years was forced to retire after his racist text messages were exposed. He referred to Black people as "niggers" and "nothing but a bunch of monkeys" and stated "I wish someone would pull a Ferguson on them and take them out. I hate looking at those African monkeys at work ... I enjoy arresting those thugs with their saggy pants." (September 2014)

CAMERON TILLMAN (14) and four other teenage friends were reported as armed men burglarizing a house. The house in question had been abandoned for years and was used by the boys as a hangout—with the owner's consent. When an officer knocked at the door, Tillman opened it and was shot on sight. A BB gun was found at the scene. (September 2014)

A White man (Derrick Daniel Thomas) robbed a home at gunpoint and then, after leaving, fired several shots at a man sitting in a truck with his 5-year-old son. After chasing him and backing him into a standoff, police said the man stepped out and pointed his gun at the officers. He was not shot. They ordered him to drop the weapon, but he reportedly answered, "No, you drop your fucking gun!" He was still not shot; he was instead arrested unharmed after trying again to flee. (April 2014)

ERVIN EDWARDS (38) and his girlfriend had concluded an altercation before police arrived. He was then arrested for violation of a unanimously passed city ordinance that requires pants "to be secured at the waist so they do not fall below the hips." At the West Baton Rouge Parish Jail, surveillance footage shows that Edwards was dragged into an isolation cell by several officers, where one held a taser to him for almost a full minute. The officers then left him face down and unresponsive in the cell for ten minutes before medical intervention was provided. (November 2013)

Two teenagers, **Sidney Newman** and **Ferdinand Hunt**, were hanging out after a Mardi Gras parade in the vicinity of Hunt's mother, an NOPD officer, who was working. Surveillance video shows that, as one sat on a wall and another leaned, at least seven White plainclothes state troopers tackled the boys to the ground. When Officer Hunt reached the scene, the boys were released to her, and the officers just walked away. State police called allegations of racial profiling absurd, stating that they were looking for juvenile violations, illegal weapons, and narcotic activity when they noticed two individuals who appeared to be juveniles and decided to ID them. (April 2013)

Local Resources

American Civil Liberties Union of Louisiana: laaclu.org, (504) 522-0617
Louisiana Commission on Human Rights:
gov.louisiana.gov/page/lchr, (225) 342-6969
Louisiana NAACP: lanaacp.org

MAINE
1.4% Black
(about 18,000 out of 1,300,000)

	Black	White
Poverty Rate	n/a	12%
Unemployment Rate	n/a	3.9%
Imprisonment Ratio	6	1

Open carry permitted: YES	Stand your ground law: NO
Active hate groups: 2	2016 election result: Democrat

Percentage of Black victims of law enforcement killings (2013-16):
0%
(0 out of 16)

Notable Incidents

Speaking about Maine's effort to combat drug crime, Governor Paul LePage said that "the enemy right now...are people of color or people of Hispanic origin. ... When you go to war...and the enemy dresses in red and you dress in blue, then you shoot at red." (August 2016)

Governor Paul LePage blamed the state's heroin problem on "guys by the name D-Money, Smoothie, Shifty" who "come from Connecticut and New York. ... They come up here, they sell their heroin, then they go back home. Incidentally, half the time they impregnate a young white girl before they leave." In a subsequent interview, he told a reporter, "Let me tell you something: Black people come up the highway and they kill Mainers. You ought to look into that." (January 2016)

> **FIND ANOTHER PLACE TO REST YOUR NIGGER HEAD.**
> —Airbnb host

A pair of White brothers was involved in an altercation with a third party. When **Antonio Byars** became the sole Black person in a crowd of onlookers, he was targeted. The brothers asked what he was looking at and then attacked him, using racial slurs while threatening to kill him. A civil rights complaint was filed by the attorney general. (April 2015)

Witnesses observed a member of a car full of young White men scream "hey, niggers" at **Shay Stewart-Bouley** and her children, including a 9-year-old daughter. (April 2015)

Local Resources

American Civil Liberties Union of Maine: aclumaine.org, (207) 774-5444
Attorney General: maine.gov/ag, (207) 626-8800
Maine Human Rights Commission: state.me.us/mhrc, (207) 624-6290
Maine NAACP: naacp.me

MARYLAND
30.5% Black
(about 1,800,000 out of 6,000,000)

	Black	White
Poverty Rate	17%	6%
Unemployment Rate	8.2%	3.3%
Imprisonment Ratio	4.7	1

Open carry permitted: YES	Stand your ground law: NO
Active hate groups: 11	2016 election result: Democrat

MARYLAND (cont.)

Percentage of Black victims of law enforcement killings (2013-16):
65.6%
(61 out of 93)

Notable Incidents

Students at a Silver Spring, MD elementary school found the message "KILL KILL KILL BLACKS" written in a bathroom. (November 2016)

Cellphone video captured a White female teacher at Harlem Park Middle School in Baltimore calling unruly Black students "idiots." She then told them, "You have the chance to get an education, but you want to be a punk-ass nigger who's gonna get shot." (November 2016)

Two instances of graffiti reading "TRUMP NATION WHITES ONLY" were found at a church in Silver Spring, MD. (November 2016)

The White sheriff of one of the wealthiest counties in the United States was forced to resign after the county's Office of Human Rights issued a 48-page investigatory report concluding that he had made remarks insulting the intelligence of Black deputies, had used racist gestures, and had often described African Americans as "niggers." He had served for ten years. (October 2016)

Black students staged a walk-out at Mount Hebron High School in Ellicott City after a racist 30-second video of a fellow student, who is White, surfaced on social media. In the video, the student disparages Black Lives Matter and says "who the fuck cares about some black man who dies? ...

They're an inferior race, OK? Does anybody really care?" He also grabs a five-dollar bill, holds it up to the camera, and asserts that Abraham Lincoln "is a traitor to the white race." (January 2016)

A White female shouted racial slurs before shooting two Black high school athletes with a BB gun. (April 2015)

FREDDIE GRAY (25) was not committing any illegal behavior but was chased and arrested on what seemed to be suspicion that he *could* have committed some. His subsequent treatment and death in custody brought to light myriad issues within the Baltimore Police Department, including routine violation of the constitutional rights of citizens, excessive use of force, and discrimination against African Americans, as determined by a subsequent U.S. Department of Justice investigation. (April 2015)

When **Towhee Sparrow, Jr.** appeared, his yellow motorbike made him close enough to the description of the suspect a White police officer sought. The officer forced Sparrow to lie on the ground with his hands behind his head and then "repeatedly slammed his knee into Sparrow's neck, back, and the side of his head while yelling racial slurs," according to a federal complaint. When a second White officer arrived, he joined in on the physical and verbal abuse, stating "You think you're tough because you pulled your gun on a white man" and suggesting that the officers should kill him right there. Shortly thereafter, witnesses to the original crime being investigated stated that Sparrow looked "nothing like" the suspect. In his lawsuit, Sparrow indicates that the incident is part of a pattern of police abuse already the subject of three previous lawsuits dating back to 2008. (June 2014)

Before exiting his car to enter his home, which he was parked in front of, **William Cunningham** began being interrogated by a police officer. When he tried to go into his house, the officer doubled back, drew his gun, and put it to Cunningham's head, commanding him to get back into his car and antagonizing him. The incident was recorded on a bystander's cellphone. The officer was later convicted of assault. (May 2014)

A White member of the Kappa Sigma fraternity at the University of Maryland sent a misogynistic and slur-filled email about rush week that included the command "don't invite any nigger gals." (January 2014)

Members of the Ku Klux Klan group the Confederate White Knights held a rally at a national park that contains a Civil War battlefield. (September 2013)

Local Resources

American Civil Liberties Union of Maryland: aclu-md.org, (410) 889-8555
Attorney General: marylandattorneygeneral.gov/pages/civil
Maryland NAACP: naacpmd.com
State of Maryland Commission on Civil Rights: mccr.maryland.gov

MASSACHUSETTS
8.4% Black
(about 572,000 out of 6,800,000)

	Black	White
Poverty Rate	17%	8%
Unemployment Rate	7.8%	3.5%
Imprisonment Ratio	7.5	1

Open carry permitted: YES	Stand your ground law: NO
Active hate groups: 4	2016 election result: Democrat

Percentage of Black victims of law enforcement killings (2013-16):
31.3%
(15 out of 48)

Notable Incidents

A car with a Confederate flag and the words "KILL KILL KILL" was spotted after the presidential election. (November 2016)

Two White male Babson College students were expelled from their fraternity after targeting Black students at Wellesley for harassment the day after the election. (November 2016)

Graffiti at Attleboro High School read "KKK will handle all niggers" and "Go Donald Trump." (November 2016)

A Ku Klux Klan-affiliated newspaper, *The Crusader*, was distributed to two neighborhoods. (November 2016)

"AMKKK KILL" was painted on a wall at Williams College. (November 2016)

A teaching assistant at Marine Biological Laboratory was expelled after threatening to burn a cross in front of a Black student's home. (August 2016)

When a group of Black teens was ejected from an MBTA train by police, 16-year-old **Jelani** was also put off, even when he pointed out that he was not with the group. When a White woman on the train objected, stating that he wasn't with the group, he was allowed back on. (July 2016)

Portraits of exclusively Black faculty members were defaced

with strips of black tape at Harvard Law School. (November 2015)

Swastikas and the word "nigger" were spray painted on the homes of two Black families who lived blocks apart from each other. (April 2015)

Racist graffiti was found in a University of Massachusetts dormitory. "KILL THESE NIGGERS!!" was written on a Black student's door, and "You guys got nigger boyfriends" was found on the door of two female students. An arrest was made. (October 2014)

Multiple discrimination complaints have been filed against the company where **Sylvester Cyler** was employed. On behalf of an Angolan co-worker who was being harassed with monkey comparisons and other racist depictions, Cyler filed a harassment charge against their White male manager. The manager then began directing threats and racist remarks to Cyler. The co-worker ultimately reached an out-of-court settlement with the company. (December 2013)

The harassment of **Isaac Phillips,** a biracial eighth grade member of his school's football team (known as the Blue Knights), culminated in an incident of vandalism when his home was spray painted with the words "KNIGHTS DON'T NEED NIGGERS." Two previous incidents involving the team also involved the use of racial slurs. (November 2013)

Local Resources

American Civil Liberties Union of MA: aclum.org, (508) 444-ACLU
Attorney General: http: www.mass.gov/ago/bureaus/public-protection-and-advocacy/the-civil-rights-division, (617) 727-8400
Massachusetts NAACP: bostonnaacp.org, (617) 427-9494

MICHIGAN
14.2% Black
(about 1,400,000 out of 9,900,000)

	Black	White
Poverty Rate	26%	9%
Unemployment Rate	12.4%	3.7%
Imprisonment Ratio	6.6	1

Open carry permitted: YES	Stand your ground law: YES
Active hate groups: 13	2016 election result: Republican

Percentage of Black victims of law enforcement killings (2013-16):
36.3%
(29 out of 80)

Notable Incidents

In response to a Black woman's comment of "Black Lives Matter" on a Facebook post that featured Colin Kaepernick taking a knee during the national anthem, a White fireman wrote: "You are the true epitome of a nigger. All lives matter. And if you think it's just black lives kiss my ass bitch and go back to the fields that us in the north fought to free you from." He was fired from his job. (December 2016)

A White man used his business's Instagram account to send racist threats to **Dominic Lebron** after determining that Lebron had an interest in his girlfriend. "Heard you'd talk to her if I wasn't in the picture? Fucking nigger Ima put you in the dirt. ... If you want a job let me know. I got mad cotton out bad [sic] that has to be picked." (December 2016)

A White woman was recorded at the polls on election day spitting in a Black man's face and repeatedly calling him and other Black bystanders nigger. (November 2016)

A White female news anchor was quoted as saying, "I'm tired of reporting on these niggers killing each other in Detroit." She subsequently resigned. (November 2016)

Two-foot high graffiti at Eastern Michigan University read "LEAVE NIGGERS." (October 2016)

After **Ashton Brooks** earned a spot as the first female player on Dow High School's football team, a White female student from a rival high school posted an Instagram picture of herself posing with someone in a gorilla costume and captioned it "Got a pic with dows kicker ;)." (October 2016)

Graffiti at Eastern Michigan University read "KKK" and "LEAVE NIGGERS." (September 2016)

White supremacist fliers were posted around the University of Michigan. One flier was entitled "Why White Women Shouldn't Date Black Men" and claimed in great detail that Blacks are abusive, disease-ridden, unintelligent, and violent. (September 2016)

In a video posted on Facebook, White Grosse Pointe High School students expressed what they would do to Black people in 2040 as President of the United States. "Stupid, worthless, need to leave our country, send 'em back to Africa," one student said. The reinstitution of slavery and segregation was proposed. "White people are gonna be the dominants of the country.

We're not gonna put 'em in coffins. We're gonna put 'em in the river and let them swim to the Atlantic Ocean." The school announced that all students involved received either suspensions or "separations." (May 2016)

An arrest was made based on a messaging app threat, "going to kill all black people," that was directed at Michigan Technical University students. (November 2015)

Despite not resisting arrest during a traffic stop, dashcam footage shows police officers putting **Floyd Dent** in a chokehold and savagely beating and tasing him. Two officers were suspended, one was charged with assault, and a large settlement was reached. (January 2015)

Newspapers from the Knights of the Ku Klux Klan were left in a neighborhood. (September 2014)

In April 2014, despite resident concerns over water quality due to sewage spills and industrial waste, officials in Flint, MI made what was to be a temporary switch to water from the Flint River instead of relying on water from Detroit in an effort to save money. Residents immediately complained about the smell, taste, and appearance of the water and raised health concerns, reporting rashes, hair loss, and other problems. In February 2015, a resident contacted the Environmental Protection Agency (EPA) with her concerns about the water. The EPA found a lead level nearly seven times greater than the allowable limit; further testing found a level almost quadruple that of the original test. Officials denied the problems, but by September 2015, a study showed that the number of children with elevated lead levels in their blood had nearly doubled and in some cases tripled. In

November 2015, residents filed a federal class action lawsuit claiming 14 state and city officials, including the governor, knowingly exposed them to toxic water. Flint's population is 56.6% African-American, and 41.2% live below the poverty line. (April 2014)

RENISHA MCBRIDE (19) had crashed her car late at night in a predominantly White neighborhood and knocked on a White man's door, ostensibly for assistance. The man opened the door and shot McBride in the face with a shotgun. He was convicted of murder and sentenced by a judge who deemed his response one of "unjustified fear." (November 2013)

Local Resources

American Civil Liberties Union of Michigan: aclu-mn.org, (651) 645-4097
Michigan Department of Civil Rights: michigan.gov/mdcr, 800-482-3604
Michigan NAACP: detroitnaacp.org, (313) 871-2087

MINNESOTA
6% Black
(about 331,000 out of 5,500,000)

	Black	White
Poverty Rate	n/a	5%
Unemployment Rate	n/a	2.9%
Imprisonment Ratio	11	1

Open carry permitted: YES	Stand your ground law: NO
Active hate groups: 3	2016 election result: Democrat

Percentage of Black victims of law enforcement killings (2013-16):
20%
(11 out of 55)

Notable Incidents

The day after the election, graffiti was placed on a Maple Grove Senior High School bathroom door reading "fuck niggers" followed by "#fuckallporchmonkeys," "#whitesonly," "#whiteamerica," and "Trump." (November 2016)

A student placed a "KKK Wants You" placard in a classroom. Disciplinary action was taken. (November 2016)

Video footage shows **Larnie Thomas** being harassed and ultimately arrested for walking in the street, which he was doing due to construction on the sidewalk. (October 2016)

PHILANDO CASTILE was the passenger in a car pulled over for a broken tail light. As per gun carry law, he informed the officer that he had a gun. When he attempted to retrieve his license, the officer shot him multiple times. The driver's 4-year-old daughter was in the back seat. (July 2016)

Because **Frank Baker** "fit the description" of a suspect, a White police officer released his dog to attack him. The dog held Baker's leg for over 70 seconds, causing extreme damage, and, while Baker writhed on the ground screaming in pain, the officer kicked him in the ribs. Baker, who was unarmed and not the suspect, sustained fractured ribs and collapsed lungs and required skin grafts for the dog-bite injuries. (June 2016)

Patrons **Tyrone Williams** and

Chauntyll Allen found a photo of a Texas lynching of two Black men embedded as art in their table at Joe's Crab Shack. The image was embellished with a speech bubble reading, "All I said was 'I don't like the gumbo!'" (March 2016)

> The enemy right now...
> are people of color...
> —STATE GOVERNOR

A young White male shot five Black people at a Black Lives Matter protest march. Text and electronic messages between him and three other White male accomplices included:
- an image of a rifle pointed at a crude, racist drawing of a Black man
- Blacks being referred to as "uneducated monkeys"
- a statement about making Black parents huddle with their children in their homes "hoping and praying that I pass them by without killing every firstborn black in the neighborhood"
- photos of swastikas, Hitler, and an image reading "Hitler did nothing wrong"
- a request that friends "come practice for when we have to shoot black guys" (November 2015)

Cell phone footage of a dispute over a parking space devolved to the White man stating "fuck you, niggers—there, I said it" and bragging that Minneapolis cops "shoot the niggers." (November 2015)

The words "Nigga Lover Bitch" were spraypainted on the apartment door of a White woman with a young biracial daughter. (January 2014)

Video footage shows **Christopher Lollie** being confronted by cops for sitting in a bank waiting area. He is harassed, tased, and ultimately arrested while a White person also seated there remains undisturbed. (January 2014)

Local Resources

American Civil Liberties Union of Minnesota: aclu-mn.org, (651) 645-4097
Minnesota Department of Human Rights: mn.gov/mdhr, (651) 539-1100
Minnesota NAACP: naacpmpls.com; naacp-stpaul.org, (651) 649-0520

MISSISSIPPI
37.6% Black
(about 1,100,000 out of 2,900,000)

	Black	White
Poverty Rate	27%	14%
Unemployment Rate	9.2%	4.1%
Imprisonment Ratio	3	1

Open carry permitted: YES	Stand your ground law: YES
Active hate groups: 14	2016 election result: Republican

Percentage of Black victims of law enforcement killings (2013-16):
47%
(24 out of 51)

Notable Incidents

White students at a south Mississippi high school put a noose around the neck of a Black student and "yanked backward." (October 2016)

A marker for the site where **Emmett Till**'s body was found was riddled with bullet holes. Signs commemorating Till have been vandalized, torn down, stolen, and shot repeatedly since they went up in the mid-2000s. Meanwhile, a marker for the home of one of Till's killers has been preserved and adorned by the planting of flowers. (October 2016)

Seminary High School's gym was vandalized with repeated instances of the word "nigger" and the phrase "KKK still alive got my eyes on you boy." The graffiti was thought to be directed toward the basketball coach. (October 2016)

At the University of Mississippi (Ole Miss), students held a sit-in to demand a reaction from the university to a student's tweet in response to North Carolina protests over the police shooting of a Black man. The student tweeted of those protesting: "I have a tree with room enough for all of them, if you want to settle this Old West Style." (September 2016)

Graffiti found in a University of Southern Mississippi bathroom contained comments disparaging African Americans and mentions of the KKK and Donald Trump. (February 2016)

An entry to a newspaper contest soliciting ideas for a new state flag included a caricature of a Black face with huge lips and a drawing of fried chicken. (February 2016)

A woman paid for a space at an RV park but was evicted the next day when the owner called her to say she hadn't divulged that she was married to a Black man. He told her, "You don't talk like you wouldn't be with no black man. If you would had come across like you were with a black man, we wouldn't have this problem right now." (March 2016)

JONATHAN SANDERS (39), who was traveling by horse, commented something to the effect of "why don't you leave that man alone" to a cop conducting a traffic stop on an acquaintance of his. The officer abbreviated the stop, stating "I'm going to get that nigger," and got back into his unit (with his wife). Once behind Sanders, he turned on his lights, which caused the horse to startle and throw Sanders. Sanders had gotten up to pursue the horse when the officer came from behind, yanked him to the ground, and placed him in a chokehold, which he maintained for at least 20 minutes. The entire time, the officer ignored bystander comments that Sanders wouldn't be able to breathe, Sanders's own statements of "I can't breathe," and an offer of CPR by a trained professional. A grand jury indictment was refused. (July 2015)

Two White women were convicted for the 2011 hate crime that resulted in the death of **James Craig Anderson.** Anderson was run over by a truck when a group of White teenagers left a party and traveled to Jackson with the intent of assaulting African Americans. Ten White teens were charged in Anderson's death. (April 2015)

A White State Representative commented to a reporter that he was against increased funding for education, in particular funding to improve literacy, because he comes "from a town where all the blacks are getting food stamps and what I call 'welfare crazy checks.' They don't work." He later apologized for the remarks. (February 2015)

A White judge was helping out at a local market where **Eric Rivers,** who is mentally disabled, was trying to earn tips from vendors by helping them unload. The judge struck Rivers across the face and yelled "run, nigger, run!" A witness stated that afterwards, he saw the judge "laughing and giving a high five to a police officer." The judge was later indicted and pleaded guilty to assault. (May 2014)

Three Ole Miss students hung a noose and a Confederate flag around the neck of a statue of **James Meredith,** who was honored for integrating the university. Two students were arrested and convicted of a hate crime. (February 2014)

Someone hung a noose holding the head of a stuffed animal outside the office of mayoral candidate **Percy Bland.** (April 2013)

Local Resources

American Civil Liberties Union of MS: aclu-ms.org, (601) 354-3408
Mississippi NAACP: naacpms.org, (601) 353-6906

MISSOURI
11.8% Black
(about 719,000 out of 6,000,000)

	Black	White
Poverty Rate	25%	7%
Unemployment Rate	9.7%	4%
Imprisonment Ratio	4.1	1

Open carry permitted: YES	Stand your ground law: NO
Active hate groups: 14	2016 election result: Republican

Percentage of Black victims of law enforcement killings (2013-16):
41.9%
(44 out of 105)

Notable Incidents

Cell phone video of a high school basketball game showed White students at the home school, Warrensburg High, turning their backs en masse and holding up a Trump campaign sign when Black students from Kansas City Center, the away team, were introduced. Warrensburg is a largely White school; Center is predominantly African American, and all of the Center basketball players in the starting lineup were Black. (December 2016)

White Ladue School District students chanting "Trump! Trump! Trump!" suggested Black students should move to the back of the school bus. Ladue is among the wealthiest communities in Missouri. Only about 1% of the town's 8,500 residents are Black, but about 20% of the student population is because it is drawn from nine additional municipalities. (November 2016)

Police were summoned to an Arnold, MO disturbance being caused by an armed White male. The man fired on police with a shotgun, sending two officers to the hospital. Police did not return fire. The man was taken into custody unharmed. (November 2016)

A group of White students at the University of Missouri (Mizzou) hurled racial slurs at two Black students as they crossed paths in front of the Delta Upsilon fraternity house. The encounter drew a crowd, and additional racial slurs were shouted from the windows of the fraternity house. The fraternity was placed on suspension. (September 2016)

Two White men drove up to a bus stop in St. Louis and began yelling racial epithets at a Black woman, including calling her a "nigger bitch," as well as throwing eggs. They were arrested and charged with a hate crime. (June 2016)

White Saint Louis University (SLU) students described President Obama as "a colored" and a "fucking watermelon eatin [sic] baboon" in a GroupMe message group comprised of SLU baseball players. Upon seeing the comments, freshman **Dominique Morgan** filed a bias incident report. (April 2016)

The embattled president of the University of Missouri System was forced to resign after appearing unresponsive to Black student concerns about racism on the campus. The resignation ended graduate student **Jonathan Butler**'s hunger strike for the cause. (November 2015)

A White man was arrested for making online threats to shoot Black students at Mizzou in retaliation for their race-based protests. One post read: "I'm going to stand my ground tomorrow and shoot every black person I see." (November 2015)

A White man interrupted a group of Black students rehearsing for a Mizzou homecoming performance and, upon being removed, stated, "these niggers are getting aggressive with me." (October 2015)

Mizzou student body president **Payton Head** reported that he was walking with a friend when a pickup truck slowed down and a group of young people inside screamed a racial epithet at him. (September 2015)

The Washington University in St. Louis chapter of the Sigma Alpha Epsilon (SAE) fraternity was suspended due to an incident involving pledges photographing a group of Black students and subsequently singing a rap song with racially offensive words in response to the photo. (March 2015)

A U.S. Department of Justice investigation of criminal justice system practices in Ferguson, MO found that nearly every aspect of their law enforcement showed bias against African Americans. The system was found to be based on revenue rather than public safety with Black residents bearing the brunt of its execution. Disproportionate justice system engagement with Blacks was found to stem from widespread departmental and agency sentiments of "bias against and stereotypes about" Black people rather than Black people actually committing more crime. A sample of evidence leading to these conclusions includes:

- Ferguson's population is 67% Black, but Blacks made up 85% of traffic stops, 90% of tickets, and 93% of arrests (between 2012 and 2014), including all arrests where "resisting arrest" was the only charge.
- Disrespectful treatment and abuse of African Americans was a routine practice of the Ferguson Police Department. At times, the racial bias was explicit in these interactions. On a domestic call, an officer threatened a Black man, saying "nigger, I can find something to lock you up on." When the Black man replied "good luck with that," he was assaulted and told "don't pass out, motherfucker, because I'm not carrying you to my car."
- When a Black man was seen resting in his car after playing basketball, an officer blocked him in, demanded identification, accused him of being a pedophile (due to children being present in the park), ordered him out of his car for a pat-down, and requested to search the vehicle. When the man objected, he was arrested at

gunpoint and charged with myriad frivolous offenses that wound up costing the man his federal employment.
- A Black woman parked her car illegally once. Inability to afford the fine and the court's refusal to accept partial payments ended up causing her to spend six days in jail as missed payments result in arrest warrants. The initial fine of $151 ballooned to more than $1,000 over time.
- Upon encountering a 14-year-old Black boy waiting in an abandoned house for friends, officers used a dog to attack him and then struck him while he was lying on the ground. Dogs were exclusively used on Black people in Ferguson.
- 88% of police use-of-force cases were against African Americans.
- In court cases, African Americans were 68% less likely than others to receive a dismissal from a municipal judge.
- In 2013, African Americans accounted for 92% of cases in which an arrest warrant was issued.
- E-mails containing racist messages were exchanged among police and criminal court staffers.

(March 2015)

After the Justice Department's Ferguson investigation turned up racist content in a quantity of work e-mail messages, a police captain and a police sergeant were forced to resign and a clerk of court was fired. The messages were primarily forwards containing disparaging jokes (e.g., a message titled "Very Rare Photo" included an image of former president Ronald Reagan feeding a baby monkey with the caption "Rare photo of Ronald Reagan babysitting Barack Obama in early 1962"). According to the DOJ, the content of the messages "demonstrate[ed] grotesque views and images of African Americans in which they were seen as the 'other'...and characterized as lacking personal responsibility" as well as "stereotype[d]...as criminals." (March 2015)

Members of a White supremacist prison gang known as the Southwest Honkies were charged with a hate crime after threatening to kill an African-American woman and her children while trying to break into her house. Five other White supremacist gangs are also known to operate in Missouri. (February 2015)

A White man was sentenced to 75 days in jail for grabbing a Black waitress and telling her he wanted to show her "where I hung your grandpa." (January 2015)

A group of demonstrators marched from Ferguson, MO to the capital to protest the police shooting of Michael Brown. When they reached the town of Rosebud (population 400), 200 angry counter-protestors shouted racial epithets. One brandished a Confederate flag and simulated a Ku Klux Klan hood. A display of fried chicken, a watermelon, and a 40-ounce beer bottle had been placed in the street. (December 2014)

The Traditionalist American Knights of the Ku Klux Klan distributed fliers around the St. Louis area threatening violent action against Ferguson "terrorists" if they became violent. (November 2014)

Fliers from the Traditional American Knights of the Ku Klux Klan were left at residences in a neighborhood. (October 2014)

A Missouri newspaper published a cartoon intended to depict unrest in Ferguson, MO over the shooting of Michael

Brown. In it, Black protestors were depicted as thieves, carrying signs that read "Steal to Honor Michael" and "No 60-inch Plasma TV, No Peace!" (August 2014)

A White St. Louis County police officer was suspended after posting an hour-long racial rant against minority groups, women, liberals, and politicians. This was the same officer who physically tried to prevent CNN's **Don Lemon** from broadcasting live at a protest over the shooting of Michael Brown. (August 2014)

MICHAEL BROWN (18) was unarmed when he was shot multiple times by a White police officer in Ferguson, MO. The incident sparked months of protests and was the catalyst for a Department of Justice review of the city's criminal justice system that exposed myriad disparities rooted in racial bias. (August 2014)

Fliers from the Knights of the Ku Klux Klan were left in a neighborhood. (October 2013)

Local Resources

American Civil Liberties Union of Missouri: aclu-mo.org, (314) 652-3111
Missouri NAACP: http: naacpmissouri.blogspot.com

MONTANA
0.6% Black
(about 6,000 out of 1,000,000)

	Black	White
Poverty Rate	n/a	10%
Unemployment Rate	n/a	3.7%
Imprisonment Ratio	6.3	1

| Open carry permitted: YES | Stand your ground law: YES |
| Active hate groups: 5 | 2016 election result: Republican |

Percentage of Black victims of law enforcement killings (2013-16):
0%
(0 out of 24)

Notable Incidents

A White coffee shop owner posted to Facebook a viral video of Black men assaulting a White man and wrote "These fucking monkeys would be hanging if I saw this shit," later adding "You don't see white people doing this shit!" After backlash, he deleted his account. (November 2016)

A White male substitute teacher engaged a high school classroom about the movie "Star Wars" and "how it related to white supremacy and the KKK." After two Latino students asked for passes to leave, other students reported that the teacher said the boys "were acting like niggers." The teacher was removed. (November 2016)

As part of a homecoming week custom of wearing colors assigned by grade level, a White high school junior wore a t-shirt with "White Power" on the front and "Trump 2016 White Pride" on the back. Another wore a white shirt with a Confederate flag. Both were included in the class picture, which was distributed widely. (September 2016)

> **KKK♥**
> —HIGH SCHOOL GRAFFITI

Fliers from the United Klans of America were left on doorsteps. (August 2014)

When a White female neighbor was accosting a non-resident for walking through the neighborhood, **Lawrence Blackwell** intervened. This prompted the neighbor to say, "I'm not talking to you, you black nigger." She began to harass him around town, yelling "nigger" whenever she saw him. Blackwell filed a restraining order. The woman violated it by trying to physically push him out of a neighbor's house, at which point Blackwell filed assault charges that were enhanced to a felony due to hate crime implications. The woman was found guilty and sentenced to a minimum of two years. (September 2013)

Local Resources

American Civil Liberties Union of MT: aclumontana.org, (406) 443-8590
Montana Human Rights Bureau: erd.dli.mt.gov/human-rights
Montana Human Rights Network: mhrn.org, (406) 442-5506
Montana NAACP: naacpstateconference.org, (844) UR-NAACP

NEBRASKA
5% Black
(about 95,000 out of 1,900,000)

	Black	White
Poverty Rate	46%	7%
Unemployment Rate	n/a	2.5%
Imprisonment Ratio	8.4	1

Open carry permitted: YES	Stand your ground law: NO
Active hate groups: 3	2016 election result: Republican

Percentage of Black victims of law enforcement killings (2013-16):
20%
(6 out of 30)

Notable Incidents

Three Black University of Nebraska-Lincoln football players took a knee during the national anthem before a football game against Northwestern as part of the Colin Kaepernick-spurred protest against incidents of racial injustice in the United States, including the killings of Black men by police officers. In response, they received social media threats including suggestions that they be "lynched or shot just like the other black people who have died recently" or "hung before the anthem before the next game." In commenting on their protest, the governor called it "disgraceful and disrespectful." (September 2016)

A White senator posted a photo of black cows blocking a roadway with the caption "Road blocked due to a black lives matter protest in the sandhills." (July 2016)

Despite signs warning against entering the water at a Disneyworld resort, a vacationing White couple from Nebraska allowed their 2-year-old to play there. The child was attacked by an alligator and died from his injuries. Unlike the Black couple whose child bypassed a barrier at the Cincinnati Zoo, resulting in the zookeeper shooting the gorilla Harambe, the White couple was not persecuted, deemed unfit, or petitioned for investigation. (June 2016)

A White Donald Trump supporter agreed to remove the "NIGGER OBAMA" sign from his window after citing that "it might be a little racist." His neighbors across the street were a Black family with two young daughters. (January 2016)

Time for a Tree and a Rope... —JUDGE

Threatening letters were being left overnight for a White woman with a Black boyfriend, **Curtis Jackson**. Messages included "dating a black man is a sin" and "you're dumb for dating a black guy, and you're gonna make dirty black babies." The culprit, a White man, was caught on surveillance footage and was seen one night by the couple, which ultimately relocated out of concerns for their safety. Upon reporting the incident, they learned that ten other interracial couples had also been receiving the letters. (July 2015)

A student at the University of Nebraska-Lincoln used the N-word and other epithets at a meeting while objecting to a proposed resolution against the use of derogatory language in their everyday speech. (November 2013)

The word "nigger" was written in chalk on a campus sidewalk at the University of Nebraska-Lincoln. (November 2013)

In retaliation for an incident in which her cousin received an in-school suspension, a White female high school student wrote the word "nigger" seven times on the car of fellow student **Isaiah Wilson**. The teen was forced to apologize by the school. (October 2013)

In response to a parking complaint, more than 30 Omaha police officers, mostly White, apprehended and beat **Octavius Johnson** and several members of his family. After a video of the incident emerged, a lengthy internal investigation occurred, and six officers were fired. (March 2013)

Local Resources

American Civil Liberties Union of Nebraska: aclunebraska.org
Lincoln Commission on Human Rights: lincoln.ne.gov/city/attorn/human
Nebraska NAACP:
iowanebraskanaacp.org; omahanaacp.org; naacplincolnbranch.org

NEVADA
9.3% Black
(about 273,000 out of 2,900,000)

	Black	White
Poverty Rate	30%	8%
Unemployment Rate	n/a	5%
Imprisonment Ratio	4.1	1

Open carry permitted: YES	Stand your ground law: YES
Active hate groups: 2	2016 election result: Democrat

Percentage of Black victims of law enforcement killings (2013-16):
13%
(9 out of 69)

Notable Incidents

A Black family reunion at a Nevada campsite was abruptly ended after a White male began berating attendees with racial slurs and ultimately charged them with what was thought to be a shotgun.

Reunion participant **Kanisha Allen** reported that "All you could hear was 'I'm going to kill you f'ing N's.'" The family, including children, was forced to run, with one elderly member sustaining an injury in the process. (September 2015)

A White Assemblywoman, speaking on behalf of a proposed voter ID law, responded to a Black colleague as follows: "But I can tell you the great respect I have for my peer Mr. Munford for being the first colored man to graduate from his college. We're in 2015 and we have a black president, in case anyone didn't notice. So the color and the race issue, I think it's time that we put that to rest." (March 2015)

JOHN T. WILSON III (22) was reported to law enforcement for carrying a "high-powered rifle." Officers responded and shot him in the back. He was holding a pellet gun. Few other details are available. Nevada has no laws prohibiting open carry. (November 2014)

A White Republican Assemblyman was forced to step down after archived writings of his emerged, one of which included this passage: "The relationship of Negroes and Democrats is truly a master-slave relationship, with the benevolent master knowing what's best for his simple minded darkies." (November 2014)

It will be so refreshing to have a classy, beautiful, dignified First Lady back in the White House. I'm tired of seeing an ape in heels.

—❖—

—FACEBOOK POST
CO-SIGNED
BY A MAYOR

A White rancher, who emerged unscathed after a now-infamous large-scale armed standoff against the federal government, stated in an interview: "I want to tell you one more thing I know about the Negro." He then recalled drives past a public housing project in North Las Vegas. "In front of that government house the door was usually open, and the older people and the kids—and there is always at least a half a dozen people sitting on the porch—they didn't have nothing to do. They didn't have nothing for their kids to do. They didn't have nothing for their young girls to do. And because they were basically on government subsidy, so now what do they do? They abort their young children, they put their young men in jail, because they never learned how to pick cotton. And I've often wondered, are they better off as slaves, picking cotton and having a family life and doing things, or are they better off under government subsidy? They didn't get no more freedom. They got less freedom." (April 2014)

DAVID L. ROBINSON (38) was walking across the street at night when a lone patrol officer decided to confront him. Robinson was homeless and tried to run. The officer followed and, within about a minute's time, had cornered Robinson and shot him three times in the head, claiming he saw "the glint of a blade." A knife was subsequently found still in Robinson's back pocket. The officer subsequently resigned. (March 2014)

Local Resources

American Civil Liberties Union of Nevada:
aclunv.org, (702) 366-1226, (775) 786-6757
Nevada Equal Rights Commission:
detr.state.nv.us/nerc.htm, (702) 486-7161, (775) 823-6690
Nevada NAACP: naacptristateinu.org, (801) 250-5088

NEW HAMPSHIRE
1.5% Black
(about 20,000 out of 1,300,000)

	Black	White
Poverty Rate	n/a	6%
Unemployment Rate	n/a	3.3%
Imprisonment Ratio	5.2	1

Open carry permitted: YES	Stand your ground law: YES
Active hate groups: 2	2016 election result: Democrat

Percentage of Black victims of law enforcement killings (2013-16):
0%
(0 out of 10)

Notable Incidents

A White woman with a young biracial son was targeted with racist vandalism acts. In three separate incidents, the words "NIGGER LOVER" were scratched into her car, the words "NIGGER GO HOME" were written on a sign on her property, and fried chicken and watermelon were thrown at her car. (October 2016)

NYU journalism graduate students **Taisha Henry** and **Ugonma Ubani-Ebere** attended a Marco Rubio campaign event in New Hampshire and were setting up to film when they were approached and told that they could not do so without a press pass. Despite putting their equipment away, they were confronted two more times; simultaneously, their White male classmate was allowed to set up for filming with no interference. (February 2016)

White festival-goers tore down street signs, started fires, threw bottles, broke into stores, and turned over cars at a small town's annual Pumpkin Festival. Though more than 30 people were injured and 84 were arrested, the media portrayed the event as "rowdy" and "boisterous" while unrest in Ferguson, MO by Blacks protesting police brutality was deemed "violent" and "criminal." (October 2014)

TO ME A REALLY GOOD HIGH IS STOMPING THE SHIT OUT OF A NIGGER FOR NO REASON.

— CORRECTIONS OFFICER

A town resident overheard the White male police commissioner refer to then-President Barack Obama as a nigger and wrote to the town manager about it. In an internal email follow-up, the police commissioner wrote, "I believe I did use the 'N' word in reference to the current occupant of the Whitehouse [sic]. For this, I do not apologize -- he meets and exceeds my criteria for such." His duties as police commissioner included hiring, firing, and disciplining officers as well as setting their salaries. He was eventually forced to resign behind the incident. (March 2014)

Several White fraternities and sororities at Dartmouth College threw a "ghetto party" in which students dressed as urban African Americans. (August 2013)

Local Resources

American Civil Liberties Union of NH: aclu-nh.org, (603) 225-3080
NH Commission for Human Rights: nh.gov/hrc, (603) 271-2767
New Hampshire NAACP: seacoastnaacp.com, (603) 436-6099

NEW JERSEY
14.8% Black
(about 1,300,000 out of 8,900,000)

	Black	White
Poverty Rate	21%	7%
Unemployment Rate	6.8%	4.4%
Imprisonment Ratio	12.2	1

Open carry permitted: YES	Stand your ground law: NO
Active hate groups: 6	2016 election result: Democrat

Percentage of Black victims of law enforcement killings (2013-16):
46.7%
(35 out of 75)

Notable Incidents

The home of NFL player **Nikita Whitlock** was broken into, burglarized, and vandalized. The perpetrator inked a swastika, the letters "KKK," and the words "Go back to Africa" on the walls. (December 2016)

The day after the 2016 presidential election, a White Allentown High School student posted a Snapchat image of Black students in a cafeteria lunch line. The student captioned the photo "Last free meal." (November 2016)

Nine corrections officers in Camden County were terminated after the contents of a batch of illicit cell phones being used by the officers were discovered. Over 5,000 text messages exposed an overwhelming morass of racism that included a suggestion that a Black Philadelphia

Eagles player "should be tied to a bumper and dragged" or doused with alcohol, set afire, and urinated on. Other examples include:
- "To me a really good high is stomping the shit out of a nigger for no reason."
- "No matter how they look at things, no matter how dressed up they get.. When they wake up tomorrow morning they're still just NIGGERS."

(November 2015)

PHILLIP WHITE (32) was the subject of a disorderly person call. Bystander video shows White on the ground on his stomach. Though White is already subdued with an officer straddling his back, a dog is released, and the officer yells "get him!" The officer punches White several times while the dog attacks him. White died on the way to the hospital. (March 2015)

A long-serving White animal control officer was forced to resign after a discrimination lawsuit exposed racist and homophobic text messages he had sent to his staff. Messages included comparing Michelle Obama to a monkey and threatening Reverend Al Sharpton with a "bullet in his head." (March 2015)

Fliers from the Loyal White Knights of the Ku Klux Klan were left on lawns. (January 2015)

A lawsuit filed by **Marcus Jeter** alleged racial profiling on the part of the Bloomfield Police Department. The suit stems from a case of wrongful arrest and police brutality that occurred in June 2012. Jeter was violently dragged from his car and punched relentlessly by an officer screaming "stop resisting" and "stop going for my gun" despite the fact that Jeter had his hands in the air. A department cover-up then ensued, with township police creating false reports. They also withheld dashcam video that corroborated Jeter's allegations. Two officers were each sentenced to five years in prison for the assault. (June 2014)

In a portion of a discussion about tax rate changes that was recorded on a voicemail, a long-serving White councilwoman is heard saying: "This is terrible. This is gonna be a fucking nigger town." She was running for mayor at the time but did not win. (April 2014)

A White woman raising two biracial grandchildren found her car damaged by vandals. All four tires had been slashed, and the words "nigger lover" had been applied in yellow spray paint. (March 2014)

The discovery of text messages riddled with racial epithets called into question a White Edison, NJ police officer's ability to deal fairly with minorities but resulted only in a temporary suspension without pay. (October 2013)

Fliers from the White nationalist group the Advanced White Society were distributed in a neighborhood. (September 2013)

A Black driver was verbally assaulted with racial slurs by a White man who had gotten out of his car in traffic. The White driver, who was later arrested, had previously been arrested for waving a Confederate flag and yelling racial slurs. (August 2013)

After a lengthy job search resulting in no responses, **Yolanda Spivey** created a new profile under a different name. All of the experience information was the same, but the answer to the diversity question on the new profile was White instead of Black. She received 16 responses within a week. (April 2013)

The letters "KKK" were written on a Black family's residence. (February 2013)

A White Glassboro High School student was charged with harassment after the discovery of a photo of two Black classmates she posted on Twitter with the caption "Stupid niggers in my algebra class...." (January 2013)

Local Resources

American Civil Liberties Union of New Jersey: aclu-nj.org, (973) 642-2084
Attorney General, Division on Civil Rights: nj.gov/oag/dcr
New Jersey NAACP: njnaacp.org

NEW MEXICO
2.6% Black
(about 54,000 out of 2,000,000)

	Black	White
Poverty Rate	39%	10%
Unemployment Rate	n/a	4.5%
Imprisonment Ratio	6.4	1

Open carry permitted: YES	Stand your ground law: NO
Active hate groups: 0	2016 election result: Democrat

Percentage of Black victims of law enforcement killings (2013-16):
3.9%
(3 out of 77)

NEW MEXICO (cont.)

Notable Incidents

A convenience store owner maintains a window covered with inflammatory signs, including an anti-Barack Obama sign that reads "2012 No Re-Nig" and an anti-Colin Kaepernick sign reading "Colin Kaeper-dick, you overpaid half-breed: Take your millions and go back to Africa." (December 2016)

A Roswell newspaper published a cartoon with a directional street sign that read "Cesar Chavez Home and National Monument 811 Miles West" and "Martin Luther King Jr. Birth Home and National Historic Site 1,272 Miles East." The cartoon was captioned, "Roswell signage suggestion...to clear up any confusion about where some people should go." (February 2015)

Local Resources

American Civil Liberties Union of NM: aclu-nm.org, (505) 266-5915
New Mexico NAACP: naacpabq.org; naacpsfnm.blogspot.com

NEW YORK
17.6% Black
(about 3,400,000 out of 19,700,000)

	Black	White
Poverty Rate	22%	10%
Unemployment Rate	7.7%	3.8%
Imprisonment Ratio	8	1

Open carry permitted: NO	Stand your ground law: NO
Active hate groups: 17	2016 election result: Democrat

Percentage of Black victims of law enforcement killings (2013-16):
47.5%
(56 out of 118)

Notable Incidents

A White male member of the Buffalo Board of Education was forced to resign after racist commentary of his regarding the Obamas was published in a local paper. He stated that, in 2017, he hoped "Obama catches mad cow disease after being caught having relations with a Her(e)ford" and that he'd like Michelle Obama "to return to being a male and let loose in the outback of Zimbabwe where she lives comfortably in a cave with Maxie, the gorilla." A board member commented that "This level of hatred for African Americans cannot and should not set policy for the education of African-American children." More than 70% of the district is not White. (December 2016)

A swastika and the words "MAKE AMERICA WHITE AGAIN" were spray-painted on the wall of a sports complex. (November 2016)

Retired Black corrections officer **Ronald Lanier** accused two White police officers of racial profiling based on a mistaken arrest. The officers, who sought a fleeing shoplifter, grabbed Lanier and, despite his attempts at cooperation and identification of himself as law enforcement, manhandled him into handcuffs. His attorney clarified: "They didn't have a good description of who they were looking for. That doesn't give you the right to go into a store and grab the first Black person you see and throw them to the ground. The fact that he happened to be a Black male in the store does not make him a culprit. It does not make him a suspect." (November 2016)

At the State University of New York at Brockport, officials were investigating the discovery of the words "niggers deserve to die" written on a whiteboard in a dormitory that houses many minority students. (September 2016)

Upon losing a free seat on the subway to a Black woman, a White man loosed a torrent of obscenities and racism toward her. Among other things, cellphone video recorded him saying "Donald Trump 2016. Put them back in the fucking fields where they belong." (July 2016)

An attempted arrest of 16-year-old **Rhamar Perkins** for jumping a subway turnstile in Brownsville, NY turned into an all-night manhunt, complete with helicopters, after he got away from police. The immense effort to catch a boy who skipped out on a $2.75 fare highlights to what extents "broken windows policing" of minorities will go. (June 2016)

The Alpha Epsilon Pi fraternity at Ithaca College advertised a "Preps & Crooks" theme party. Attendees were instructed to dress in preppy style or to come as "crooks," which "refers to a more '90's thuggish style. Come wearing a bandana, baggy sweats and a t-shirt, snapback, and any 'bling' you can find!" They also boasted "we'll have 30 gallons of jungle juice." (October 2015)

SUNY Plattsburgh's college paper, *Cardinal Points*, ran a cover story entitled "Minority Admission Rates Examined," which was accompanied by a caricature of a Black person in a cap and gown walking down a street that featured graffiti, broken and boarded up windows, a damaged street sign, and a car on cinder blocks. (October 2015)

Queens resident **Cynthia Jordan** was hailing a cab outside of Macy's in Herald Square with her daughters. When a cab stopped to drop off passengers, they tried to get in, but the driver told them he was going on break. Jordan took his number to report him because his light was still on, indicating that he was on duty. Moments later, her daughter pointed out the same driver picking up two White women up the block. Jordan ran over and confronted him, at which point he told her, "Go ahead; report me." She did, and he was ultimately fined $25,000. (August 2015)

SAMUEL HARRELL (30), who was suffering from bipolar disorder, was having a mental episode in which he believed his family had arrived to fetch him from prison. The resulting confrontation with corrections officers found Harrell thrown to the floor, handcuffed, and beaten to death by as many as 20 officers—including members of a group known around the prison as the Beat Up Squad. Harrell was repeatedly kicked and punched, with some of them shouting racial slurs, according to more than a dozen inmate witnesses. The officers filed a report accusing Harrell of being high on synthetic marijuana and stating that he "ended up deceased." A toxicology screen showed no drugs in Harrell's system. (April 2015)

AKAI GURLEY (28) was shot dead in an unlit housing project stairwell by a police officer who had drawn his gun in advance of the "vertical patrol." Gurley had committed no crime and was unarmed; he and his girlfriend had entered the stairwell because the elevator was out of order. The incident raised discussion around the "broken windows" preventive policing approach being applied in many urban minority communities. (November 2014)

Fliers from the Loyal White Knights of the Ku Klux Klan were left in two neighborhoods. (September 2014)

Two young Jewish men attacked and beat **Dieuphene Hyppolite,** who was 56, when he went out to walk his dog. The men threw garbage cans at him and punched him in the face several times, saying "fuck you, you fucking nigger!" (August 2014)

Fliers from the Loyal White Knights of the Ku Klux Klan were left on the driveway of residents in a local neighborhood. (August 2014)

ERIC GARNER (43) had committed no offense when NYPD officers, summoned by a prior altercation between other parties, decided to arrest him on suspicion of one. He voiced his objections, and a White officer put him in a chokehold and wrestled him to the ground in response. Bystander video shows that about five cops held him down as he said repeatedly, "I can't breathe." Despite the chokehold being both the primary cause of death and a maneuver expressly prohibited by NYPD regulations, a grand jury refused to issue an indictment. (July 2014)

When **Narvell Benning** started his car to leave the parking lot of a store in Buffalo, a White woman and her children were standing nearby. The children were startled, which prompted the White woman to call him a nigger. At that point, he started recording her with his cell phone. The woman got her husband on the phone and said to him, "Talk to this fucking nigger right now." She went on to call Benning a nigger several more times: "I called you a nigger. You're a NIGGER. NASTY FUCKING NIGGER." Her children, observing in the background, appeared to be about 4 and 7 years old. (June 2014)

Swastikas and the words "Hile [sic] Hitler," "FUCK NIGGERS," and "DIE NIGGERS" were scrawled on a statue of Jackie Robinson outside the Brooklyn Cyclones stadium. (August 2013)

DEION FLUDD (17) was in a subway station in a predominantly Black area when he squeezed through a turnstile with his girlfriend on a single MetroCard swipe. He was already in the system for minor offenses—possession of marijuana, fighting in school, turnstile jumping—and knew that a new offense, despite its triviality, would find him sentenced as an adult by virtue of his age. So when the cops appeared, he fled. According to the police, he was hit by a train in the process. Fludd was paralyzed from the neck down and died two months later. His death highlights the perils of a system that over-polices at the disproportionate expense of minorities. (May 2013)

After **Trayon Christian** purchased a $350 belt at Barneys, he was stopped by undercover officers that asked "how a young black man such as himself could afford to purchase such an expensive belt?" Despite showing the officers the receipt for the belt, his ID, and the debit card used, officers accused him of using fake identification and arrested him. He later sued Barneys, which settled out of court for more than half a million dollars. (April 2013)

After **Kayla Phillips** used her tax return money to buy a $2,500 purse at Barneys, she was surrounded and detained by police at the subway station. Multiple allegations of racism against the store resulted in a 2014 settlement that included a $525,000 penalty and mandatory implementation of a slate of anti-discrimination policies. (February 2013)

Local Resources

NAACP Legal Defense Fund: naacpldf.org, (212) 965-2200
New York Civil Liberties Union: nyclu.org, (212) 607-3300
New York State Division of Human Rights: dhr.ny.gov

NORTH CAROLINA
22.1% Black
(about 2,200,000 out of 10,100,000)

	Black	White
Poverty Rate	24%	10%
Unemployment Rate	9.6%	4.7%
Imprisonment Ratio	4.3	1

Open carry permitted: YES	Stand your ground law: YES
Active hate groups: 19	2016 election result: Republican

Percentage of Black victims of law enforcement killings (2013-16):
40.8%
(58 out of 142)

Notable Incidents

Yanceyville, NC hosted a "National Klonvocation"—a meeting of Loyal White Knights from around the country—in preparation for the next day's Klan-sponsored demonstration in celebration of the election of Donald Trump. (December 2016)

Students at Wake Forest University reported that one or more people ran around residence halls shouting "nigger" following the election results. A statement from the university said, "University police are responding to a bias report about a racial slur and have identified two suspects in a single incident. They are working with the person who reported the offensive behavior." (November 2016)

In the wake of increased African-American voter participation—and after state laws crafted to address this issue were struck down as discriminatory—one county in North Carolina challenged the legitimacy of 138 voters just weeks before the election. Of the 138 challenged, 92 were Black, including **Grace Hardison**, who was 100 years old at the time and had lived in the county her entire life. (November 2016)

A wall in Durham was defaced with the words "Black Lives Don't Matter and Neither Does [sic] Your Votes." (November 2016)

Attendees at the Alpha Phi Alpha statewide convention at the Sheraton and Koury Convention Center found huge graffiti of the word "NIGGER," the letters "KKK," and a swastika scrawled on the exterior of a bathroom stall. (November 2016)

When North Carolina State University sophomore **Marcus Lowry** was added to a GroupMe group called "Sullivan Squad," he scrolled back to read the full thread. It was there that he found numerous racial comments from his suitemate, a White male freshman, and other

White students. Comments included:
- "BLM is the cause of all the issues and shit. BLM is practically a terror organization, promoting killing cops, looting stores, and burning down buildings."
- "Bruh we in the private chat you can call a nig a nig"
- "They aren't fans of dumb black niggers I guess, what racists"
- About a protest in Charlotte: "Let me guess. Women's rights (which should never happen), black lives matter (they don't), or gender discrimination (even though there's only 2 genders)?"
- About a Black Lives Matter protest: "So the monkey exhibit got let out" (September 2016)

A White police officer was fired after attention was brought to this Facebook post made by him:

> You are NOT victims anymore
> You are the bad guys now
> You have your hand out for more freebies
> You won't take responsibility for yourself
> You have a 74% illegitimacy rate
> You are 13% of the population but you commit 65% of the crime
> You produce nothing
> You contribute nothing
> You take and just want more
> You don't think the laws should apply to you
> You blame others for your own decisions
> You don't try in school
> You don't try at work
> You have no concept of personal responsibility
> You don't see the direct connection between your own decisions and the impact on your quality of life
> You can't imagine how hard it is to make it in the world, because you never try
> You think you can have quality of life without earning it
> You don't raise your children with any morality
> You celebrate violence and misogyny
> You defend the inexcusable
> You beat your domestic partners
> You think you are owed

126

something, when you're not
At this point you are not victims of the bad guys,
You ARE the bad guys.
(September 2016)

Speaking with regard to protests following the police shooting of **Keith Lamont Scott,** a North Carolina state representative said: "The grievance in [the protesters' minds] is the animus, the anger—they hate white people because white people are successful and they're not." (September 2016)

KOUREN-RODNEY THOMAS (20) was attending a party when he was shot by a White man who called 911 to report "a bunch of hoodlums out here racing." The man told the dispatcher "I am locked and loaded. I'm going outside to secure my neighborhood." In a 911 call placed after the shooting, he referred to the "hoodlums" in question as "frigging black males." (August 2016)

Portions of North Carolina's 2013 voting law, which was widely considered the strictest in the nation, were struck down by a federal court of appeals as "target[ing] African Americans with almost surgical precision." Among other things, the law imposed photo identification requirements and did away with early voting and out-of-precinct voting options. These changes disproportionately affected poor, elderly, and Black voters, who were less likely to hold the required forms of photo ID, more likely to move frequently, and more likely to take advantage of early voting. The judge wrote: "The General Assembly enacted [these changes] in the immediate aftermath of unprecedented African-American voter participation in a state with a troubled racial history and racially polarized voting. The district court clearly erred in ignoring or dismissing this historical background evidence, all of which supports a finding of discriminatory intent." (July 2016)

A White man in Wake County, NC was reported for pointing a shotgun at passing motorists. When an officer arrived, the man pointed the shotgun at him and was not shot. The officer instead grabbed the end of the shotgun and kept the man from firing. The man then retrieved a handgun from his pocket, clearly intending to shoot the officer, and he was still not shot. The officer wrestled the handgun from the man as he fired. The man was arrested unharmed. (July 2016)

A hospital employee was fired after posting Facebook comments saying that Black people are "dead weight on the American economy" and that "when it comes to taking care of their children even dogs have more parental instincts than most blacks." (June 2016)

A Black woman had booked an Airbnb stay in Charlotte, but the homeowner canceled the booking. His message to her was: "I hate niggers so I'm gonna cancel you- This is the south darling. Find another place to rest your nigger head." (June 2016)

Cell phone video captured a White police officer who pulled over two Black men in an affluent neighborhood, asserting that they weren't supposed to be there. The men actually owned a house for sale in the area and were able to escort the officer there and offer him a tour of the $300,000 home. (June 2016)

After protestor **Rakeem Jones** was elbowed in the face by a White attendee at a Fayetteville Trump rally, police arrested Jones. When the White man was later interviewed, he said Jones deserved it and "the next time we see him, we might have to kill him." (March 2016)

White students at West Brunswick High School initially hung a Confederate flag at lunchtime. It was then taken down, and a White male student wrapped it around his neck like a cape and ran through the cafeteria, stomping on chocolate milk cartons and yelling "White power" while being high-fived by other students. Video of the incident was posted to Instagram. (March 2016)

Fliers from the Karolina Knights were distributed throughout a town. (April 2015)

The North Carolina State University chapter of the Pi Kappa Phi fraternity was suspended after the discovery of their pledge book, which was filled with handwritten racist and misogynistic comments, including, "You can only trust a nigger as far as you can throw them" and "Man that tree is so perfect for lynching." (March 2015)

A 52-year-old White man was charged with ethnic intimidation and assault after a traffic dispute turned into an attack on a Black woman because of her race. (January 2015)

Fliers from the Traditionalist American Knights of the Ku Klux Klan were left in driveways in two towns. (January 2015)

> We ain't taking no niggers here.
> —FIRE DEPARTMENT CHIEF

A White male sent a raft of racist threats to Raleigh's first African-American female police chief, **Cassandra Deck-Brown**. His messages included threats of beheading and indiscriminate killing of Black people, including the message "you people deserve to die." Email subject lines included "Resign Nigger," "Black Trash," and "I will kill you." (October 2014)

When a neighbor saw 18-year-old **DeShawn Currie** enter the home where he lived as a foster child of a White family, they assumed it was a break-in and called the police. (October 2014)

Fliers from the Loyal White Knights of the Ku Klux Klan were left in a neighborhood. (July 2014)

The GOP precinct chair in a North Carolina county gave an interview about North Carolina's new voter legislation in which he said: "I don't think any part of the law is racist. ... If it hurts the whites so be it. If it hurts a bunch of lazy blacks that want the government to give them everything, so be it." He was later fired. (October 2013)

JONATHAN FERRELL (24) had crashed his car and was subsequently killed by police, who were called after he knocked on the door of a house in a White neighborhood to ask for help. (September 2013)

In the parking lot of an ABC store, **Christopher Beatty** was waiting for a friend and drinking an Arizona Iced Tea when he was approached by an undercover police officer. The plainclothes officer asked Beatty what he was drinking and if it had alcohol in it. Beatty indicated that it did not and showed him the can; the White officer, who only then identified himself as a cop, insisted that he surrender it to him. Beatty refused, and the officer first attempted to eject him from the premises and then arrested him for trespassing. Beatty was ultimately cleared of the charges, but it took 18 months and cost him his job. (April 2013)

Local Resources

American Civil Liberties Union of North Carolina:
acluornorthcarolina.org, (919) 834-3466
North Carolina NAACP: naacpnc.org, (919) 682-4700

NORTH DAKOTA
2.4% Black
(about 18,000 out of 758,000)

	Black	White
Poverty Rate	n/a	9%
Unemployment Rate	n/a	2.3%
Imprisonment Ratio	5.2	1

Open carry permitted: YES	Stand your ground law: NO
Active hate groups: 1	2016 election result: Republican

Percentage of Black victims of law enforcement killings (2013-16):
0%
(0 out of 6)

Notable Incidents

White University of North Dakota students posted social media photographs of themselves imitating blackface with charcoal skincare masks twice in a 48-hour period. One instance included the caption "Black Lives Matter." (September 2016)

A group of University of North Dakota students posted images of themselves to Snapchat after reportedly locking a Black student out of her own dorm. The photo, which shows three laughing White female students, was posted with the caption, "Locked the black bitch out." (September 2016)

Red River High School students donned KKK-style robes and hoods at a hockey game. Administration stated that action was taken against the students. (February 2013)

Local Resources

American Civil Liberties Union of North Dakota: aclund.org

OHIO
12.7% Black
(about 1,500,000 out of 11,600,000)

	Black	White
Poverty Rate	34%	10%
Unemployment Rate	10.8%	3.6%
Imprisonment Ratio	5.6	1

Open carry permitted: YES	Stand your ground law: YES
Active hate groups: 14	2016 election result: Republican

Percentage of Black victims of law enforcement killings (2013-16):
43.2%
(54 out of 125)

Notable Incidents

A Cincinnati-based interracial couple found their home demolished by vandals who spray-painted "DIE NIGGER" and "WHITE POWER" on the walls along with swastikas. The vandals also tore down railings, poured paint into the appliances, ripped out walls, poured cement down the drains, broke open the pipes, and left the water running to cause flooding damage. (December 2016)

In an away game at Wapakoneta High School, the Trotwood-Madison High School marching band was pelted with mini-footballs and subjected to racist verbal abuse by the Wapakoneta student section. According to the Trotwood-Madison band chaperone, as they attempted to get the band out of the stadium following the game, "boys on bikes were riding around circling our buses while holding the Confederate flag. They did this at least three times before a police officer started chasing them off. We loaded as fast as we could and waited for the football team to load so we could all leave safely, and we were able to leave without any other issues." (November 2016)

A student at Shaker Heights High School posted a racially offensive Snapchat story. A friend asked her about it in a text exchange, probing whether the girl felt Black people should have equal rights. The reply was, "No because they don't work for it and as a culture they are scary, violent, rude and needy...They expect to be catered to. Like have you seen, heard the black people in the hall? They are loud, rude and annoying...they don't try they don't give a flying crap." The friend and another girl shared the messages on social media in an attempt to expose racism; both of them were suspended for "disruptive behavior." The original poster was not disciplined. (November 2016)

A fifteen foot wide caricature

of Barack Obama with the title "Obama the Nigger King" was found on the Loveland Bike Trail. The word "TRUMP" was also painted nearby. (November 2016)

A White female student at Xavier University in Cincinnati sent out a Snapchat photo of herself simulating blackface with the caption, "Who needs white when black lives matter." (October 2016)

At Xavier University in Cincinnati, a life-sized plastic skeleton was dressed in an African dashiki and posed in a dormitory window to suggest a lynching. A Trump banner reading "Make America Great Again" hung next to it. (October 2016)

Ohio University student Black Lives Matter supporters interrupted a homecoming game with chants and a "Make Racists Afraid Again" banner. Their actions were a commentary on the school's graffiti wall having been defaced with racist imagery at least four times over the preceding few months. (October 2016)

Trump's campaign chair in Mahoning County was forced to resign after making these statements in an on-camera interview:

"I don't think there was any racism until Obama got elected. We never had problems like this. I'm in the real estate industry; there's none. Now with, you know, with the people with the guns and shooting up neighborhoods and not being responsible citizens—that's a big change, and I think that's the philosophy that Obama has perpetuated on America. And if you're black and you haven't been successful in the last 50 years, it's your own fault. I think that, when we look at the last 50 years, where are we? And why? We have three generations of all still having unwed babies, kids that don't go through high school, I mean, when do they take responsibility for how they live? I think it's due time, and I think it's good that Mr. Trump is pointing that out. You've had the same schools everybody else went to. You had benefits to go to college that white kids didn't have. You had all the advantages and didn't take advantage of it. It's not our fault, certainly."

She also called the Black Lives Matter movement "a stupid waste of time" and said lower voter turnout among African Americans could be related to "the way they're raised." (September 2016)

At Ohio University, a "free speech wall" caused controversy when students found the words "Build the Wall" (in reference to one of Donald Trump's campaign promises) and a drawing of a person hanging by a noose from a tree. (September 2016)

Prior to a high school football game, **Rodney Axson, Jr.** heard his own teammates referring to players from the majority-Black rival team as niggers. He confronted them and then decided to take a knee during the national anthem in protest. The next night, at a party, a note reading "Fuck Rodney Nigger Nigger Nigger Let's Lynch Niggers" was delivered to Axson via Snapchat. (September 2016)

At the University of Dayton, a racial slur appeared on the door of a dormitory room shared by two Black students. (September 2016)

After calling him a nigger, two White men beat **Adrian Williams** with a broomstick and their fists, leaving him with a broken eye socket. The incident was captured on surveillance video. (May 2016)

A Black toddler bypassed a barrier at the Cincinnati Zoo

and fell into the gorilla pit, resulting in zookeepers having to put down a male gorilla named Harambe. Unlike myriad other incidents of White children straying into zoo enclosures, the parents in this case, **Michelle Gregg** and **Deonne Dickerson**, had their criminal history investigated, were demonized in the media, and were the subject of petitions requesting that criminal charges be brought against them. (May 2016)

A White male Pickerington High School student shared a Snapchat video of himself holding a rifle and saying "You guys ready to go nigger hunting?" (April 2016)

In the course of an assault investigation, a White man (Christopher Laugle) pointed a fake gun at an officer. According to court documents, the officer did not know the gun was fake and felt threatened. The man was not shot. Despite resisting arrest, he was apprehended unharmed. (February 2016)

University of Toledo student **Rayshawn Watkins** attended a party at his campus's Pi Kappa Phi fraternity house. In a dispute over fallen Christmas lights, members of the fraternity yelled racial slurs, punched, and kicked him. The fraternity and six students were subsequently placed on one year of disciplinary probation. (January 2016)

Several 911 calls were received about a White man (Daniel Kovacevic) walking around Akron with an assault rifle and a pistol. The weapons were real and loaded; Kovacevic, who is White, was not shot. (December 2015)

In response to a #BlackLivesMatter bulletin board being torn down in an Ohio University residence hall in November, the Black

Student Union decided to paint one of the graffiti walls on campus with the black power fist and the hashtag #BlackLivesMatter. Five days later, the group learned that it had been defaced with phrases including "Wake up you neo-progressive fucks," "Everyone goes through their own shit," and "Seriously fuck you." The word "Black" in Black Lives Matter was also crossed out and replaced with the word "All." (December 2015)

While attempting to visit his brother in Ohio for a birthday party, **John Felton** found himself being followed by a White police officer for over two miles. When the officer finally pulled him over, Felton recorded the encounter. The officer stated that he had pulled him over for not turning his turn signal on early enough before a turn. When Felton probed him as to why he had followed him in the first place, the officer replied, "You made direct eye contact with me and held onto it when I was passing you." (August 2015)

SAMUEL DUBOSE (43) was pulled over by a University of Cincinnati police officer for a missing front license plate. He started the car back up while the officer was trying to open the door, at which point the officer shot him in the head. The officer initially claimed that he fired because he was being dragged, but body camera footage proved otherwise. He was fired and indicted for murder. (July 2015)

Two sheriff's deputies were reportedly fired after racist text messages they'd sent were exposed, for example:
- "Watching history channel on MLK. Showing old films of restaurants in the south. It would have been fun to beat up coloreds cause they came into your restaurant."
- "What do apples and black

people have in common? They both hang from trees."
- "[President Obama is a] half-breed... Just because a nigger scammed the election and is pres. It does not give the G-damn right to shop at DLM."

In reality, the officers were not fired but were granted disability retirement. (February 2015)

TAMIR RICE (12) was in a park alone playing with a BB gun. A 911 caller said, "There is a guy with a pistol. ... It's probably fake, but he's pointing it at everybody." A police car raced up to within feet of Rice, and an officer jumped out of the car and shot him. Despite the breaches of protocol in handling what was believed to be an armed suspect, no charges were filed against the officers. (November 2014)

JOHN CRAWFORD III (22) was walking around Walmart talking on the phone with his girlfriend and absentmindedly carrying and twirling a toy rifle he had picked up from a shelf. After he was reported to police as menacing customers with a real gun that he had loaded, two officers arrived and shot Crawford on sight. Despite the fact that Ohio is an explicitly open carry state, a grand jury refused to indict the officers. (August 2014)

A White man in a Walmart saw John Crawford III walking around talking on his cellphone and absentmindedly carrying a toy rifle. He called 911 and reported Crawford as someone menacing customers and children by loading a gun, "waving it around," and "pointing it at people." The police arrived and shot Crawford on sight, which sent a nearby shopper into cardiac arrest. Both Crawford and the shopper died. The man was not charged for the false report. (August 2014)

After a White man was "disrupted" by the playing of his Black neighbor's children, they apologized. However, the neighbor's anger was racially motivated. In the ensuing confrontation, the White man hurled racial epithets before firing shots from a .22-caliber rifle at the neighbors' car, hitting the back window and trunk several times. He later pleaded guilty to ethnic intimidation and firearm charges. (June 2014)

An African-American student told his science teacher at Fairfield Freshman School that he would like to become president. The teacher, who is White, told him, "We do not need another black president." It was not the teacher's first racial commentary incident. (December 2013)

A teacher was forced to retire after making this Facebook post: "I don't mind if you come from the ghetto to trick or treat. But when you whip out your teeny dicks and piss on the telephone pole in front of my front yard and a bunch of preschoolers and toddlers, you can take your nigger-ass back where it came from. I don't have anything against anyone of color, but niggers stay out." (October 2013)

Fliers from the Loyal White Knights of the Ku Klux Klan were left on the windshields on cars that were parked downtown. (October 2013)

Rather than accept food stamp assistance for all of Ohio, the governor limited waivers to a handful of primarily rural and majority White counties. Urban regions with large minority populations and unemployment rates far above average were denied the assistance. (September 2013)

Oberlin College suspended classes after a student reported seeing a person dressed as a Ku

Klux Klan member near the college's Afrikan Heritage House. The sighting was one in a series of hate incidents on the campus, with 15 hate-related events having been reported in a single month. Other incidents included swastika graffiti, posters containing racial slurs, a large Nazi flag, a "whites only" sign written above a water fountain, and fliers containing racist, anti-Semitic, and homophobic language. A pair of students identified as being at least partly responsible deemed the acts "a joke." (March 2013)

Local Resources

American Civil Liberties Union of Ohio: acluohio.org, (216) 472-2200
Ohio Civil Rights Commission: crc.ohio.gov, (614) 466-2785
Ohio NAACP: naacpcolumbus.org, (614) 382-6900

OKLAHOMA
7.8% Black
(about 306,000 out of 3,900,000)

	Black	White
Poverty Rate	n/a	10%
Unemployment Rate	n/a	3.6%
Imprisonment Ratio	4.5	1

Open carry permitted: YES	Stand your ground law: YES
Active hate groups: 1	2016 election result: Republican

Percentage of Black victims of law enforcement killings (2013-16):
29.2%
(35 out of 120)

Notable Incidents

Two students were removed from the University of Oklahoma campus after carrying a banner reading "BLM ARE RACIST THUGS" on one side and "BLM RENT A RIOT" on the other. (November 2016)

Fliers titled "Why White Women Shouldn't Date Black Men" and "Race and Intelligence: the Facts" were posted at the University of Oklahoma. The first flier contains such phrases as: "He's much more likely to abuse you," "He's much more likely to have STDs," and "You should probably just avoid black men." The second includes: "In the U.S., the average white IQ is about 100, the average black IQ is about 85, and the average East Asian IQ is about 105." (November 2016)

Three people in Tulsa using the name "Daddy Trump" added Black students at the University of Pennsylvania to GroupMe groups called "Nigger Lynching," "Mud Men," and "Trump is Love." The students also received an event invite titled "Daily Lynching" in a message thread that contained a picture of a mass lynching. (November 2016)

TERENCE CRUTCHER (40), who had ingested PCP, had stopped his car in the middle of a road and gotten out. When police arrived, he was disoriented, walking away, as they followed, with his hands in the air and a vacant stare. As he reached his vehicle and allegedly put his hand through its driver-side open window, one of the officers tased him, but another shot him dead. Helicopter footage of the incident included audio of the pilot stating, "That looks like a bad dude" before Crutcher was shot. Crutcher had no weapon. (September 2016)

A retiring Black teacher was to be honored for his service at the CareerTech Summer Conference. When he took the stage, a White teacher, who was also heard making several racist comments, presented him with a white robe, a hood, and a Confederate flag. (August 2016)

Over the course of a year and a half, an Oklahoma City Police Department patrol officer preyed on low-income and exclusively Black women with criminal records as a vulnerable group lacking in credibility. He would run background checks to find information (e.g., an outstanding warrant) and then would use it against them to coerce sex and ensure their silence. His last victim, **Jannie Ligons**, who was passing through the impoverished area he was targeting, only fit the profile by her race and gender; she was neither poor nor did she have a criminal record. Ligons reported the assault immediately, and a dozen other women came forward as a result. The officer was charged with rape, sexual battery, forcible oral sodomy, and other crimes. He was sentenced to 263 years in prison. (December 2015)

The mayor of Lahoma, OK issued an apology after a photo surfaced showing her husband participating in a fake KKK rally complete with white robes and hoods, torches, and a cross. The incident was deemed a "Halloween prank." (November 2015)

ERIC HARRIS (44), who was unarmed, had attempted to

flee a sting operation for a nonviolent offense when he was shot by an armed though unofficial deputy who mistook his own pistol for a taser. While on the ground, Harris said, "He shot me! He shot me, man. Oh, my God. I'm losing my breath," to which one of the three White officers replied, "Fuck your breath. Shut the fuck up!" The deputy was later found guilty of manslaughter. (April 2015)

I have a tree with room enough for all of them...
— COLLEGE STUDENT

White members of the University of Oklahoma chapter of the Sigma Alpha Epsilon (SAE) fraternity were recorded singing the following chant:
There will never be a nigger in SAE
You can hang him from a tree, but he'll never sign with me
There will never be a nigger in SAE

The chapter was suspended, and two students were expelled. (March 2015)

Fliers from the Traditionalist American Knights of the Klu Klux Klan were distributed in a neighborhood. (January 2015)

JEREMEY LAKE (19) was dating a White girl. Her father was a Tulsa police officer who, upon learning of the relationship, looked up Lake's address, drove to his home, and waited out front in his vehicle. When Lake and the girlfriend arrived, he shot Lake multiple times, claiming that he was acting in self-defense because Lake was armed with a semi-automatic weapon. Lake was not in possession of a gun, and his aunt testified that her nephew was reaching out to shake the officer's hand to introduce himself when he was shot. (August 2014)

DANIEL MARTIN (47) was a decorated Army veteran who informed the dispatcher that he was lawfully armed when he called 911 to report vandals in his driveway. The dispatch reflects that "reporting party has a firearm." When Martin answered the door for the officers, one shouted "gun," and the officers opened fire, striking Martin with at least nine bullets. (March 2014)

To avoid the death penalty, a White man and a man claiming to be Native pled guilty to first degree murder and hate crimes based on their 2012 Tulsa shooting spree exclusively targeting African Americans. Three Black men were killed and two others were wounded. (December 2013)

Local Resources

American Civil Liberties Union of Oklahoma: acluok.org, (405) 524-8511
Attorney General: ok.gov/oag/About_the_Office/OCRE.html
Oklahoma NAACP: okcnaacp.org, (405) 236-2227

OREGON
2.1% Black
(about 86,000 out of 4,100,000)

	Black	White
Poverty Rate	n/a	10%
Unemployment Rate	n/a	5.5%
Imprisonment Ratio	5.6	1

Open carry permitted: YES	Stand your ground law: NO
Active hate groups: 4	2016 election result: Democrat

Percentage of Black victims of law enforcement killings (2013-16):
4.2%
(3 out of 70)

Notable Incidents

Two White students from Oregon City High School (OCHS) posted a Snapchat of themselves having the following conversation:
- "What do you think about niggers?"
- "Tom Lovell [Principal of OCHS] is a fucking nigger who arranges five niggers a day coming into the school at OCHS. Fuck him!"
(December 2016)

Two bathrooms at Reed College's library were defaced with racist, homophobic, anti-Semitic, and pro-Trump graffiti, including:
- WHITE IS RIGHT
- FUCK ALL YOU LIBERAL NIGGERS DIE
- FUCK BROWN LOW-IQ AFFIRMATIVE ACTION
(November 2016)

The sole Black female student at Clackamas Academy of Industrial Sciences, **Joy Simmons,** received harassing notes based on her race, including one that read "Go back to Africa Nigger." (November 2016)

A Black student at OCHS, **N'Dea Flye,** received a note on her doorstep that read: "Go back to picking cotton Nigger BlackLivesDoesn'tMatter" (October 2016)

In a picture posted on Twitter, former and current White students from OCHS held a sign reading "Welcome back to the farm Nigger" with a drawing of a Ku Klux Klan member. (October 2016)

A University of Oregon student

saw and recorded three teenagers wearing blackface on campus. (October 2016)

Many called for the resignation of a law professor from the University of Oregon after she attended a Halloween party in blackface makeup with an afro wig. (October 2016)

Three young Hispanic brothers on a MAX train filmed an incident in which **Nitasha Sweaney**, who was riding the train with her child, was harassed by a White man after she refused to give him money. He screamed "Fuck you, fucking nigger" at her before turning his attention to the boys. "Film me, nigger," he said, before swinging at the phone. (August 2016)

A police officer was placed on leave after Facebook posts promoting violence against Black Lives Matter protests were discovered. One post read, "When encountering such mobs remember, there are 3 pedals on your floor. Push the right one all the way down." Another post, regarding a national day of protest for Black Lives Matter, was captioned: "So Day of target practice?" (July 2016)

While walking her dog, **Christiana Clark** was confronted by a man yelling, "It's still an Oregon law—I could kill a black person and be out of jail in a day and a half. Look it up. The KKK is still alive and well here." The man was known as a serial perpetrator of racially based verbal attacks. (June 2016)

A White woman left notes on the door of **Elizabeth Philips** and text messages with a neighbor after she felt Philips had parked too close to her car. Messages included:
- "We are Not the same species."
- "Ape gots the cops here...idk why. Probably because she's

a nigger getting' in trouble."
- "Apes were never meant to drive so stop!"
- "U look like a monkey & you smell like one too!!!"
- "I've been here 22 years and no niggers and now you. U made me hate niggers now."
- "I'm not racist but I can see how someone can become hating niggers. You did this. There were no niggers in W.L. until u came." (April 2015)

Local Resources

American Civil Liberties Union of Oregon: aclu-or.org
Oregon Civil Rights Division: oregon.gov/boli/CRD
Oregon Coalition Against Hate Crime: oregoncahc.org/report-a-hate-crimeincident
Oregon NAACP: naacpaowsac.org

PENNSYLVANIA
11.7% Black
(about 1,500,000 out of 12,800,000)

	Black	White
Poverty Rate	25%	9%
Unemployment Rate	10.4%	4.3%
Imprisonment Ratio	8.9	1

Open carry permitted: YES	Stand your ground law: YES
Active hate groups: 23	2016 election result: Republican

Percentage of Black victims of law enforcement killings (2013-16):
30.6%
(33 out of 108)

PENNSYLVANIA (cont.)

Notable Incidents

A student at Highlands High School shared a Snapchat photo of a "FEDERAL NIGGER HUNTING LICENSE." (December 2016)

School administration was informed by a motorist that the word "nigger" and a swastika were inscribed in the condensation of an East Penn School District bus window. (December 2016)

Black students at the University of Pennsylvania were added to GroupMe groups called "Nigger Lynching," "Mud Men," and "Trump is Love." They also received an event invite titled "Daily Lynching" that contained a picture of a mass lynching. (November 2016)

The principal of Southern Lehigh High School had to issue a statement regarding racial incidents at the school, including Black students being called cotton pickers and niggers, swastikas being carved into bathroom stalls, and students giving "Heil Hitler" signs. The statement explained that an assembly had been held at the school to address the issues and requested that parents continue the conversation in their homes. (November 2016)

In Philadelphia, an SUV was spray-painted with the words "Trump Rules" and "Black Bitch." (November 2016)

The day after the election, cellphone video emerged of White students at a high school parading the halls with a Trump sign and at least one student calling out "White power!" (November 2016)

A White teenager at Saucon

Valley High School recorded a Black fellow classmate eating chicken wings and posted the video to Snapchat. The White student narrated over the video, calling the Black student "a nigger eating chicken" in addition to other uses of the N-word and references to him being broke and on welfare. (October 2016)

A White man posted a video of an altercation between himself and a Black woman who had been sitting on the steps of the Pennsylvania Academy of Fine Arts, which had been employing him as an art model. He called the woman a "shit-colored shaved ape," "ghetto monkey," "monkey face," and "gorilla" in addition to telling her "you're inferior" and "you belong in a cage." He was fired and banned by the school. (October 2016)

An Instagram photo featured several White female students from Central Dauphin School District posing with a handwritten sign that read "You stupid nigger." (October 2016)

In a Snapchat video, a White female student at Albright College simulated blackface, called herself "Carlisha," and stuffed the seat of her pants in mockery of Black women. (September 2016)

Calls for resignation arose after Facebook posts from the mayor of a Pennsylvania town came to light. The posts included:

- an image of several apes in a wheelbarrow with the caption, "Aww...moving day at the Whitehouse [sic] has finally arrived." Lettering superimposed on the wheelbarrow reads "Kenya or bust"
- an old movie still of Clint Eastwood holding up a noose with the caption, "Barry, this rope is for you. You wanna bring that empty chair over here!"
- a photo of a smiling monkey

with the caption, "Most think it is Obama's picture......sorry its [sic] Moochelles baby photo" He was forced to resign. (September 2016)

A White female part-time cop posted a Snapchat photo of herself in uniform with the caption "I'm the law today nigga." She was fired. (September 2016)

At an anti-fracking protest, **Tom Jefferson** was filming when a White male passerby began heckling the protestors. He turned his attention to Jefferson, calling him, "This chimp right here. Yeah, chimp. A fucking nigger right here with a fucking mop on his head." Protestors objected, to which the man replied, "I don't give a fuck. He's milking my fucking tax dollars" and then made monkey noises at Jefferson. (December 2015)

A newly-sworn White police chief in Farrel, PA had previously sent this email during a book drive fundraiser: "Good morning, Please click and review. Even $1.00 will be greatly appreciated. Them [Town of] Sharon niggas gotta learn how to read." He defended this, stating that he does "use the N-word very often because that's just the way that it is here [in] our area." (November 2015)

Three Bucknell University students were expelled after making comments including "black people should be dead" and "lynch 'em" during a campus radio broadcast. (April 2015)

A vandal defaced the sign at the country's oldest historically Black university, making it read: "Lincoln N*gger University." (February 2015)

BRANDON TATE-BROWN (26) was shot under highly questionable circumstances during a Philadelphia traffic stop in a White part of town. The officers involved offered inconsistent stories about how Tate-Brown came to be shot once in the head. His mother's pending wrongful death lawsuit calls on the court to require 91 recommendations for reform that the U.S. Department of Justice made in a May 2015 report on Philadelphia's police-involved shootings, which have averaged nearly one a week since 2007. (December 2014)

When a woman outside of his sister's Pittsburgh home cried out for help, the **Rev. Reginald Myers**, who was 65, came out only to find himself attacked by her and her two male accomplices, all of whom were White. He was beaten, kicked, and cut with a knife while the assailants screamed racial slurs. Said Myers, "He looked me square in my face and said, 'fuck you, nigger—we'll kill you.'" Myers required more than 100 stitches to his face. (November 2014)

Members of the Traditional Rebel Knights of the Ku Klux Klan held a rally. (June 2014)

Fliers from the Loyal White Knights of the Ku Klux Klan were left on cars and posted throughout a neighborhood in two different cities. (April 2014)

Members of the Confederate White Knights of the Ku Klux Klan held a rally at the Gettysburg National Military Park. (November 2013)

About 40 White supremacists attended a Philadelphia rally to celebrate Leif Erikson Day (in honor of the Norse explorer believed to have led the first Europeans to set foot in continental North America). Groups represented included the Keystone State Skinheads, which sponsored the event, the Vinlanders Social Club, the

Advanced White Society, the Blood and Honour Social Club, and the Traditionalist Youth Network. (October 2013)

Fliers from the Traditionalist American Knights of the Ku Klux Klan were left in driveways. (August 2013)

Local Resources

American Civil Liberties Union of Pennsylvania: aclupa.org
Pennsylvania Human Relations Commission: phrc.pa.gov
Pennsylvania NAACP: pastatenaacp.org

RHODE ISLAND
7.9% Black
(about 83,000 out of 1,000,000)

	Black	White
Poverty Rate	23%	8%
Unemployment Rate	n/a	4.4%
Imprisonment Ratio	8.3	1

Open carry permitted: NO	Stand your ground law: NO
Active hate groups: 1	2016 election result: Democrat

Percentage of Black victims of law enforcement killings (2013-16):
40%
(2 out of 5)

Notable Incidents

Prior to the election, **Madison Amelia** surreptitiously recorded her then-boyfriend, who is White, on a rant that included

the following:
- On the Black Lives Matter movement: "That's what Trump should do the second he's elected—give all you motherfuckers tickets back. You don't like it? Peace! Black Lives Matter? Go matter to fucking Ghana."
- On Bernie Sanders's support of Black Lives Matter: "You're a dumb fucking nigger in my book; you have no fucking value to me."
- When told his language was inflammatory: "Then don't be a dumb nigger. Don't be a dumb fucking nigger. Don't be your average fucking shoe shine boy. Get a job. Go to work. Do something other than sitting there making fucking videos about 'fuck Donald Trump gonna take my mom's fucking food stamps away and blah blah blah blah blah...I'ma start a war...I'ma go to war.' Why don't you get a fucking job, you fucking nigger. Jesus Christ. I can sound like a racist all I fucking want; I'm right."
(November 2016)

Five Black students at Providence College were turned away from an off-campus party and had beer bottles thrown at them as White students were allowed to enter. When the Black students contacted police to report an assault, the police were dismissive, citing the complainant as "person annoyed" and asserting intoxication, despite adult bystander reports to the contrary. (January 2016)

> THIS BATHROOM IS NOT TO BE USED BY FUCKING NIGGERS.
> —High School Graffiti

Fliers found in a neighborhood read: "'The nigger has the New Black Panther Party and the White Man has the Ku Klux Klan. Now ride to the sound of the guns and let's get this settled once and for all.' –

Militant Knights of the Ku Klux Klan" (October 2015)

Despite the longstanding church use of a building purchased by **Rev. Chris Abhulime** for the expansion of King's Tabernacle, he was denied such use without applying to the town's zoning board for a special use permit—which the town summarily denied. In a phone call recorded by a contractor, a zoning board official referred to Abhulime as the "fucking Black owner." Abhulime filed a lawsuit, and his attorney received an anonymous letter that read, in part: "The reason why the Revernd [sic] is having a difficult time in Johnston RI is obvious. ... We don't want any more worthless, drains on society, ill-mannered, disrespectful niggers in this town. ..." (July 2015)

A neighborhood received racial propaganda fliers claiming the White race is endangered. The fliers were delivered in plastic bags weighed down with rocks. (June 2015)

Local Resources

American Civil Liberties Union of RI: riaclu.org, (401) 831-7171
Attorney General:
riag.ri.gov/CivilDivision/OfficeoftheCivilRightsAdvocate.php
Department of Human Services: dhs.ri.gov/CivilRights/index.php
Rhode Island Commission for Human Rights:
richr.state.ri.us, (401) 222-2661
Rhode Island NAACP: naacpprov.org, (401) 521-6222

SOUTH CAROLINA
27.6% Black
(about 1,300,000 out of 4,900,000)

	Black	White
Poverty Rate	27%	9%
Unemployment Rate	9.9%	3.7%
Imprisonment Ratio	4.3	1

Open carry permitted: NO	Stand your ground law: YES
Active hate groups: 8	2016 election result: Republican

Percentage of Black victims of law enforcement killings (2013-16):
34.6%
(27 out of 78)

Notable Incidents

While shopping at a beauty supply store, **Larrishia Stanley** was called "nigger" by a White employee. When Stanley started videotaping, the woman gave her the middle finger. The employee was subsequently fired. (November 2016)

Emmy-winning TV reporter **Steve Crump** had his cameraman film a White man who had racially harassed him during a taping. When Crump asked the man what he had called him, the man verified that he had called him a nigger and a former slave. The man then asserted a claim to First Amendment rights and spoke about the Constitution. When Crump rightfully challenged his knowledge, the man replied, "You're a fucking idiot. You're ignorant. So you really are a nigger, then." (October 2016)

Three firefighters were fired after making Facebook posts calling Black Lives Matter protesters "dumb asses" and threatening to run them over. (July 2016)

When **Arthur Hill**, a recent New York transplant, entered a local barbershop asking to be served, the owner told him he doesn't do Black hair and displayed a gun. (May 2016)

Sixteen-year-old **Shakara** refused to stand and leave her math class after the teacher reportedly caught her using her phone. Video shows the school cop that was summoned violently slamming, dragging, and handcuffing the child. (October 2015)

CYNTHIA MARIE GRAHAM-HURD (54), SUSIE JACKSON (87), ETHEL LEE LANCE (70), DEPAYNE MIDDLETON-DOCTOR (49), CLEMENTA C. PINCKNEY (41), TYWANZA SANDERS (26), DANIEL SIMMONS (74), SHARONDA COLEMAN-SINGLETON (45), and MYRA THOMPSON (59) were killed when a White gunman, who had sat in their prayer meeting at Emanuel African Methodist Episcopal for nearly an hour, opened fire. Three others were shot but survived. The shooter was an avowed White supremacist who, when asked why he was perpetrating the act, stated, "I have to do it. You rape our women and you're taking over our country. And you have to go." Upon apprehension, the shooter told police he was hungry, so they stopped at Burger King for him on the way to jail. (June 2015)

WALTER SCOTT (50) was shot and killed after running away from a White police officer during a traffic stop for a nonfunctioning brake light. Scott was unarmed. The officer claimed he had shot in self-defense, but cellphone video footage showed that he had fired as Scott, who was hit in the back eight times, was fleeing. (April 2015)

A White University of South Carolina student was suspended after a photo of her writing a list on a whiteboard was shared on social media. The title of the list was "reasons why USC WiFi blows," and the first entry was "niggers." (April 2015)

The car driven by **Lakeya Hicks**, with **Elijah Pontoon** as passenger, had valid temporary tags. Though there is nothing illegal about this, White police officers cited it as the reason for a traffic stop. They then asked Pontoon for identification, though he was not the driver. Pontoon was then ordered out of the car, handcuffed, and told "You gonna pay for this one, boy." Officers brought in a drug-sniffing dog, searched the car, and, finally, conducted a roadside body cavity search.

No contraband was recovered. The encounter was recorded on dashcam video and is the subject of a federal lawsuit. (October 2014)

A state trooper pulled **Levar Jones** over for a seatbelt violation. After Jones exited the vehicle, dashcam footage showed the officer saying, "Can I see your license, please?" When Jones turned back to his vehicle to retrieve it, the officer screamed, "Get out of the car!" and fired several shots, hitting Jones once. The officer was fired. (September 2014)

The Empire Knights of the Ku Klux Klan held a rally. (July 2014)

Fliers from the Loyal White Knights of the Ku Klux Klan were distributed in a neighborhood. (July 2014)

ERNEST SATTERWHITE (68) was shot five times after not

pulling over for a police officer who suspected him of DUI. Satterwhite, who was unarmed, continued to drive for 12 miles, all the way to his house. After he pulled into his driveway and stopped the car, an officer involved in the chase charged over and shot him to death through the open window. A grand jury refused a manslaughter indictment, and a subsequent charge of misconduct resulted in a plea deal for three years of probation. (February 2014)

Local Resources

American Civil Liberties Union of South Carolina: aclusc.org
South Carolina Human Affairs Commission: schac.sc.gov
South Carolina NAACP: scnaacp.org

SOUTH DAKOTA
1.8% Black
(about 15,000 out of 865,000)

	Black	White
Poverty Rate	n/a	8%
Unemployment Rate	n/a	1.5%
Imprisonment Ratio	4.8	1

Open carry permitted: YES	Stand your ground law: YES
Active hate groups: 2	2016 election result: Republican

Percentage of Black victims of law enforcement killings (2013-16):
0%
(0 out of 14)

Notable Incidents

In response to a post by a Kansas State University student simulating blackface, a volunteer firefighter in South Dakota commented, "Think we should make slaves again" and "Vote Trump! Fuck these people." He was dismissed from his role. (September 2016)

Two vendors sold racist targets at a gun show. The targets featured a caricatured silhouette of a Black person running. The logo on the target read "Official RUNNIN' NIGGER Target." When asked about the offensiveness of the item, one of the vendors replied, "I sold 500 of them this weekend, so what difference does it make?" Both vendors were ejected and banned. (March 2015)

Local Resources

American Civil Liberties Union of South Dakota: aclusd.org

TENNESSEE
17.1% Black
(about 1,100,000 out of 6,600,000)

	Black	White
Poverty Rate	21%	13%
Unemployment Rate	8.2%	4.8%
Imprisonment Ratio	3.7	1

Open carry permitted: YES	Stand your ground law: YES
Active hate groups: 26	2016 election result: Republican

TENNESSEE (cont.)

Percentage of Black victims of law enforcement killings (2013-16):
21.6%
(21 out of 97)

Notable Incidents

In a fit of road rage, a White motorist followed **Brandon Levston** into a parking lot, where Levston recorded the following exchange:

- Driver: What's up, buddy?
- Levston: Oh, now I'm a buddy?
- Driver: Hey, Trump. Trump all the way. Trump! Hey, check this out—
- Levston: I was a nigger a minute ago; now I'm a buddy.
- Driver: Nah, I got you, because black lives don't matter. There ain't no proof. Just because you say something don't mean nothing. Prove it.
- Levston: Wow. I appreciate you. I appreciate you for sharing that.
- Driver: Hey, check it out. If black lives matter—hey, I'm talking for you. Oh, you appreciate it?
- *(both talk over each other for a couple of seconds)*
- Levston: So black lives don't matter because you got a problem in traffic?
- Driver: No. Black lives don't matter—no, the problem in traffic was you were right behind me, sped up, and drove around me, jumped in front of me, and made me slam on my brakes at a light. That makes you a nigger. That proves that black lives don't matter. Hey—no, no, no. If you have a side...if you have a subject, you tell me why black lives matter. Because people say so? You need to tell me why. Do you know what "matter" means? It's something that makes a difference. And let me tell you something—
- *(both talk over each other for a couple of seconds)*
- Driver: Hey, Martin Luther King died for a purpose. You need to watch the very first episode of "Boondocks" because he walks around ashamed of the

people with the flat-brimmed hats, like you, and the people that can't even keep their pants up. Yeah, put it on Facebook; I don't care! Look at me.
- Levston: Apparently you don't.
- Driver: You're a punk who lives off social media. I don't even have a social media account. You know why? Because white lives matter.
- Levston: I appreciate you sharing with me your life story, sir.
- Driver: What life story?
- Female passenger in White driver's car: Why don't you go put your own fucking people's lives in danger?
- Driver [to woman in car]: Hey, let me handle it. You just be a woman. *(He closes the car door.)*
- Driver: What was my life history? Was there anything of anybody's past? Or are you just another nigger who doesn't understand anything?
- Levston: Apparently you were teaching me about black people.
- Driver: I'll teach you anything.
- Levston: Teach me a little bit more about black people.
- Driver: Black people were bought by a contract, and we got ripped off. Because y'all

should've got returned when there was evidence and proof that y'all couldn't do anything because y'all live off welfare.
- *(both talk over each other for a couple of seconds)*
- Driver: Let me answer your question, nigger.
[...]
- Driver: ...I've already told you what a nigger is. It's people who have flat-billed hats, can't keep their pants up, and put people's lives in danger on the streets—cutting them off in traffic. That's a nigger. Someone who—they don't matter.
- Levston: OK.
- Driver: I have a family in my car, and you know what? We matter. Because, you know what I mean? You're going around putting people's lives in danger, and then you want to follow people and put them on social media.
- Levston: I didn't follow you, sir.
- Driver: Hey, spread this. It's OK. Spread this. People need to—hey, I'm looking at the camera now, not you. Black lives do not matter because black people walk around and say it. That don't mean anything. I could walk around and say

"Elvis is still alive," does that mean he is still alive? No. You have to prove something with your life, for once. You have to prove something, buddy. Go out and do that.
- Levston: I appreciate you so much.
- Driver [said while walking back to his car]: Yeah, you fucking transgender faggot.
- Levston [begins to drive off]: Wow.
- Driver [turns back around and begins grabbing his crotch]: That's right, BLM doesn't matter. Drive off, sucker.
[...]
- Levston [to camera]: That's exactly why y'all need to get out and vote. If you ever needed proof of why you need to get out and be heard, go fucking vote.

When asked about the incident, several of the White motorist's neighbors defended both him and his statements. (November 2016)

The deputy director of the Shelby County Corrections Center resigned after several offensive and racist statements he posted to his personal Facebook page were discovered, including the comment "The KKK is more American [than] the illegal president," posted in response to an article that suggested that then-President Obama had called Donald Trump an "agent of the Klan." (November 2016)

When Deputy **Jessica White** queried a White officer as to whether he kept full insurance on his car, he replied that he did "just in case a nigger like [her]" hit his car and had no insurance. When she was later making an inquiry about filing a grievance, the officer walked in and repeated his comment when asked. He was later suspended. (November 2016)

A White East Tennessee State University student attended a peaceful Black Lives Matter march wearing a gorilla mask and attempting to hand out bananas wrapped with nooses.

The student was arrested. (September 2016)

A White freshman at Belmont University posted a Snapchat photo of three Black NFL players with their fists raised during the national anthem. The student added the caption "Piece of shit niggers. Every one of them needs a damn bullet in their head. If you don't like this country get the hell out." The student was later expelled. (September 2016)

A customer at a restaurant discovered that she had been the target of a viral Snapchat posted by her waitress. In reference to **Chelsea Mayes** and her group, the White server posted a picture of herself with her face screwed up angrily and the caption, "I'm so hungover and have a section full of niggers right now." The waitress was later fired. (July 2016)

An active White nationalist running for congress in eastern Tennessee posted a billboard touting the phrase "Make America White Again" and another that depicted the White House ringed with Confederate flags and bore the caption "I Have a Dream." (June 2016)

Two Memphis police officers were suspended after posting a Snapchat that featured a photograph of a White hand pointing a gun at an emoji of a running Black man. (June 2016)

Police surveillance video captured a 67-year-old White woman pulling a gun on 52-year-old **James Crutchfield** after he asked her for a light for his cigarette. "It scared me absolutely to death," the woman told a reporter. "I have never been so afraid of anything in my whole life, I don't think." She was arrested for aggravated assault. (November 2015)

Three White men were sentenced for burning a cross in front of the home of an interracial family in 2012. (February 2015)

A gym owned by **Jo Williams** was defaced with a racial slur. She had previously received a note on her car referencing the KKK. (January 2015)

A White woman (Julia Shields) dressed in body armor drove around her town shooting at people. When police located her, she led them on a chase. When she was finally stopped, "she *pointed her firearm at an officer*," [emphasis added] according to a release. In lieu of being shot dead, "she was taken into custody without incident or injury." (December 2014)

You gonna pay for this one, boy.
—POLICE OFFICER

Several prominent racist leaders and around a hundred supporters of one of the largest Ku Klux Klan groups in the United States held a summit in east Tennessee at a taxpayer-funded state park resort facility with an armed park ranger on duty to provide security. (November 2014)

A cross was burned in the parking lot of a predominantly Black church. (July 2014)

The American Renaissance, a longstanding White supremacy organization, held its annual conference in Dickson, TN, where permit applications for anti-racist demonstrations were denied. This was the organization's second year using the location for their conference, whose speakers included Klan members, neo-Nazis, Holocaust deniers, anti-immigrant activists, etc. (April 2013)

A Ku Klux Klan rally was held in downtown Memphis in protest of the renaming of three parks that had honored the legacy of slavery and the Confederacy. (March 2013)

Ku Klux Klan recruiting fliers were left in driveways. (January 2013)

Local Resources

American Civil Liberties Union of Tennessee: aclu-tn.org, (615) 320-7142
TN Human Rights Commission: tn.gov/humanrights, (615) 741-5825
Tennessee NAACP: tnnaacp.org, (731) 660-5580

TEXAS
12.5% Black
(about 3,400,000 out of 27,800,000)

	Black	White
Poverty Rate	23%	8%
Unemployment Rate	7.6%	3.6%
Imprisonment Ratio	4	1

Open carry permitted: YES	Stand your ground law: YES
Active hate groups: 26	2016 election result: Republican

Percentage of Black victims of law enforcement killings (2013-16):
23.2%
(97 out of 419)

Notable Incidents

When told by her son that a White neighbor had "grabbed and choked" him for littering, **Jacqueline Craig** called the police. Bodycam footage of the event shows that, upon arrival, the officer walked past the Black complainants and instead addressed his inquiry to the White neighbor. When he then spoke to Craig, she explained that the neighbor had told her he acted against her son after the child defied him with regard to picking up the litter. At this point, the officer said, "Well, why don't you teach your son not to litter?" He then argued with her that the action was defensible because her son had broken the law and chastised her repeatedly for raising her voice. After threatening to arrest her for her tone, he produced a stun gun and wrestled Craig to the ground, arresting her and her two daughters, one of whom was a juvenile. (December 2016)

After the election, two White men assaulted a Black man at a convenience store. One of the men told the victim he was a "Trump supporter" then grabbed him by the dreadlocks, put him in a headlock, and began punching the victim in the face repeatedly. He and the other man, who also punched the victim in the face several times, were arrested. (November 2016)

The San Antonio Police Department posted a Facebook arrest report on **Otis Tyrone McKane,** who was a suspect in a police officer's murder. Under the photo, a White judge from the area wrote: "Time for a tree and a rope..." (November 2016)

After the election, threatening letters to residents were distributed in a neighborhood. They read as follows:

> OUR NEW PRESIDENT DONALD J TRUMP IS GOD'S GIFT TO WHITE NATION. WE WANT TO GET OUR COUNTY BACK ON THE RIGHT TRACK. WE NEED TO GET RID OF MUSLIMS, INDIANS, BLACKS AND JEWS.

WE CAN START WITH THE GREAT STATE OF TEXAS AND PRESIDENT TRUMP WILL TAKE CARE OF THE COUNTRY. THESE FOREGIENERS [sic] ARE TAKING OUR HIGH PAYING JOBS AND LEAVING US STRANDED. SO PLEASE DO NOT SELL OR RENT YOUR HOMES TO THEM. WE ARE EVERYWHERE AND WATCHING EVERY MOVE. WE HAVE OUR MEMBERS IN THE LAW ENFORCEMENT AND GOVERNMENT SO DON'T BOTHER GOING TO THEM.
(November 2016)

Fliers warning White women not to date Black men were discovered in residence halls at Southern Methodist University. The fliers claimed Black men are more likely to have STDs and abuse women and that "Your kids probably won't be smart." (November 2016)

Threatening fliers were posted around Texas State University. They read: "Now that our man TRUMP is elected and republicans own both the senate and the house -- time to organize tar & feather VIGILANTE SQUADS and go arrest and torture those deviant university leaders spouting off all this Diversity Garbage." (November 2016)

A White female student at Abilene Christian University posted a Snapchat video of herself simulating blackface and saying, "I am a strong black woman" before putting on a pair of bright red oversized plastic lips. Several people laughed in the background. The caption on the video read "this is why black lives matter exists." Two students were suspended. (November 2016)

After a White customer questioned **Ernest Walker**'s

military service based on him wearing his 25th Infantry Division cap indoors, the manager at Chili's, who was also White, accosted Walker and took away his free Veterans Day meal. After the incident was publicized, Walker began receiving racially-charged threats by phone, mail, and electronically, eventually prompting him to move away for the safety of his family. (November 2016)

When a passenger became unresponsive on a flight, Houston-based **Dr. Tamika Cross** offered assistance, but a flight attendant dismissed her, telling her they were "looking for actual physicians." After a page for doctors was issued by the captain, Dr. Cross offered again and was met with a request for her credentials. Her service was rejected again when a White male doctor showed up. (October 2016)

A White female student at Prairie View A&M posted a Snapchat of her face covered in black tape with the caption "When you just tryna fit in at your hbcu." (September 2016)

An employee at a Sonic was fired after putting the word "NIGGA" onto **Tyrone Moseley**'s receipt instead of his name. Moseley's friend's receipt was labeled "MEXICAN." (September 2016)

Nearly two dozen "White Lives Matter" protesters—some armed with assault rifles—staged a rally outside the Houston office of the NAACP. In addition to guns, protestors carried Confederate flags, wore White supremacist symbols, and—in at least one instance—held a sign bearing the White nationalist slogan "14 Words." (August 2016)

When a conflict arose between a Black family and a White family in a restaurant, the daughter of the Black family started a Facebook Live stream. When called racist, the White family called the Black one "Goddamn niggers" and added: "You're a fucking nigger," "All lives matter," "Take your fucking nigger ass back to Africa, ho," and "My ancestors owned your motherfucking ancestors." (July 2016)

A White female applicant who was denied admittance to the University of Texas blamed it on affirmative action and took her case to the Supreme Court. She claimed she didn't get into the school while African-American students with lower grades and test scores did. However, of the 47 students admitted with grades lower than hers, 42 were White. Further, 168 Black and Latino applicants with better grades than hers were also rejected. (June 2016)

After being pulled over for an alleged traffic violation, the officer's conduct made **Earledreka White** fearful, so she called 911 to request another officer. He subsequently arrested her. (March 2016)

A White couple (Earl Davis Williams and Kayleigh Anne Davis) was stopped on suspicion of involvement in nearby attempted burglaries. The officer saw that they were armed, and then the pair fled. During the chase, the couple began firing at the officers until they crashed and fled on foot. When officers caught up to the male, he did not comply with commands and resisted officers. He was not shot. The female was also apprehended safely. (March 2016)

A group of Black and Hispanic high school students were touring Texas A&M as prospective students when a White female college student asked two of the Black female high schoolers their opinion of her Confederate flag earrings. A nearby group of White college students joined in, telling the visiting group that they should "go back where you come from" and hurling racial epithets. (February 2016)

CALIN ROQUEMORE (23) was so afraid of police that, when one tried to pull him over for speeding on a country road after dark, he fled. He eventually jumped out of the moving car and fled on foot. An officer chased on foot and shot him seven times after Roquemore, who was unarmed, failed to put his hands up. (February 2016)

DAVID JOSEPH (17) ran unarmed and completely naked toward a police officer who was standing just inside the open door of his car. The officer, who shot Joseph three times, was fired as a result of the incident. (February 2016)

A now-closed Sara Lee factory in Texas settled a major lawsuit with 72 Black employees who stated that White supervisors had "berated" them with racial slurs, including the N-word, and that vulgar racial graffiti including "KKK" was allowed to remain as well as ape effigies hanging from nooses. Factory supervisors were also accused of assigning Black employees to positions where they developed cancer from asbestos and black mold exposure more often than their White co-workers, who were routinely promoted out of those jobs. (December 2015)

A federal appeals court dismissed **Lawanda Fennell-Kinney**'s case against a Texas school system despite pages of incidents, evidence, and previous complaints about abuse and harassment suffered by her children in their school, including a noose and note she personally found one day when she went to retrieve something from her daughter's car during school hours. The note read:

> Die Fuckin "nigger sisters" ... Bitches!!!! You can never bring our families down ... Whites will always rule this town and school!!!! Damn Spooks!!!! So go ahead and file your stupid damn complaints and grievances ... NIGGERS ... and that "Nigger Lover" you have a baby with ...

The school had put on a racial sensitivity assembly and done some extra training but refused to sign a resolution provided by the U.S. Department of Justice regarding the school's policies. The appeals court judge ruled that the school's response had been sufficient. Fennell-Kinney withdrew her children from the district. (October 2015)

Several Southern Methodist University White sorority members contributed to a post confirming that they won't accept Black members. Reasons given included:

- "[Black women are] often unqualified for recruitment (low GPA, bad grades, not involved on campus, know nothing about the houses) and ... generally come from a completely different background (impoverished lower class)."
- "[Black women] are aesthetically unpleasing to the eye for both actives and the fraternity men we associate with. No, we don't want to be the house that took 'the black' and end up like Gamma Phi, where guys avoid them like the plague. Sorry, but looks matter."
- "Y'all go to crappy high schools and generally don't deserve to even be at SMU to begin with."

(October 2015)

> Black Lives Don't Matter and Neither Does Your Votes
> —GRAFFITI

CHRISTIAN TAYLOR (19) was high when he broke into a car dealership and started jumping on the cars. A single officer, who arrived and proceeded without backup, thought he saw a bulge in Taylor's pocket and shot him four times. The bulge was a wallet and a cellphone. (August 2015)

SANDRA BLAND (28) was pulled over for failure to signal a lane change. The Black Lives Matter activist displayed an increasing level of irritation with the officer, which he deemed grounds for threatening and ultimately arresting her. She was found hung in a jail cell three days later. (July 2015)

Cops were summoned to a disturbance at a pool party with around 100 teens, most of whom were Black. As White officers chased terrified Black teens, a White teenage boy was allowed to walk around freely, filming with his cell phone. He captured footage of an officer manhandling Black teenage boys, telling them to "get your asses down on the ground" and handcuffing some. The officer then threatened and cursed a group of Black girls standing nearby and ultimately grabbed bikini-clad **Dajerria Becton**, 15, and slammed her to the ground. When Black teenage boys protested, he pulled a gun and moved quickly toward them before returning to wrest Becton to the ground again, where he grabbed her by the back of the head and pressed her face to the ground, holding it there with his knee in her back as she cried. The officer resigned, and a federal lawsuit is pending. (June 2015)

Dashcam footage with audio shows **Breaion King** asking a White police officer who had pulled her over into a parking lot for speeding if he could "please hurry up." He then forcibly removed her from the driver's seat, pulled her across a parking space, and hurled her to the asphalt. In a separate recording after the arrest, a White officer tells her that Whites may be concerned about interacting with Blacks because they can appear "intimidating." (June 2015)

In a recorded encounter, three open-carrying White men refused to comply with repeated police officer orders to put down their weapons, instead yelling back commands that the officers "calm down" and "stop threatening" them. They were not shot. (June 2015)

After **Meka Muller** posted a negative review of her Dallas apartment complex on their Facebook page, they posted, as reply: "NIGGER." (April 2015)

Police were called to the scene of a White woman (Kasi Jones) driving erratically and cursing people. She led officers on a car chase before being stopped by spike strips, at which point she emerged, refused to comply, and assaulted an officer. She was not shot. (September 2014)

CHARLES GOODRIDGE (53) was shot twice in the stomach after a struggle with an off-duty constable who had previously ejected Goodridge from the property, from which he had been evicted. Goodridge was then left bleeding on the ground for 15 minutes with no first aid administration. Dashcam footage shows that at one point, after being rolled roughly onto his stomach to be handcuffed, he raised his head, and an officer used his foot to keep Goodridge's face on the pavement. (July 2014)

Fliers from the Original Knight Riders Knights of the Ku Klux Klan were distributed in a neighborhood. (July 2014)

JASON HARRISON (38) was

schizophrenic, and his mother had called the police for help getting him to the hospital. Bodycam footage shows her step out of the house and away from the door. Her son then stands in the doorway obliviously twiddling a screwdriver. The officers immediately ask him to "drop it" then scream for him to do so, and then they shoot him five times, including twice in the back. (June 2014)

Fliers from the Loyal White Knights of the Ku Klux Klan were left at residences in a neighborhood. (March 2014)

YVETTE SMITH (47) called 911 for help because an argument between two men in her home was getting out of hand. She was a mere bystander to the dispute. When the police showed up, both men were already in the front yard, and it appeared the dispute was settled. When Smith opened the front door of her home, an officer shot her with an assault rifle. The department then issued complete fabrications about the circumstances, stating that Smith had a gun and did not comply with orders. A judge found the officer not guilty of murder. (February 2014)

JORDAN BAKER (26) was shot by a cop who told his supervisors that he stopped Baker, who was riding a bicycle at a shopping center, because he fit the description of people accused in recent burglaries. Baker, who was wearing a hoodie, was an unarmed and employed college student. A grand jury did not indict the officer. (January 2014)

LARRY JACKSON, JR. (32) had arrived at a bank intending to try to pass a bad check. When a White officer was alerted, he spoke with Jackson, who eventually fled. The officer chased the unarmed Jackson and eventually commandeered a civilian driver's car. The woman testified that he was fuming and inarticulate but that he told her Jackson wasn't dangerous. After the officer saw Jackson again, he pursued him on foot to an isolated area and ultimately shot him in the back of the neck, claiming it was an accident. The officer was charged with manslaughter but freed on a technicality. (July 2013)

Surveillance video shows two White male police officers slam **Keyarika Diggles**'s head into a countertop and yank her to the floor by her hair in the town lockup, where she was already restrained in handcuffs. The incident, which occurred in Jasper, TX (renowned for the brutal White supremacist slaying of James Byrd, Jr.), resulted in the firing of the two officers involved. (May 2013)

Local Resources

American Civil Liberties Union of Texas: aclutx.org, (713) 942-8146
Texas Civil Rights Project: texascivilrightsproject.org
Texas NAACP: texasnaacp.org

UTAH
1.3% Black
(about 39,000 out of 3,000,000)

	Black	White
Poverty Rate	n/a	8%
Unemployment Rate	n/a	3.2%
Imprisonment Ratio	7.3	1

Open carry permitted: YES	Stand your ground law: YES
Active hate groups: 2	2016 election result: Republican

UTAH (cont.)

Percentage of Black victims of law enforcement killings (2013-16):
6.7%
(3 out of 45)

Notable Incidents

Witnesses heard a White man "loudly making racist comments to another neighbor's child" as the boy rode his scooter in a common area of their apartment complex. After the boy's father heard the man tell his son "get out of here, nigger," he confronted the man, who reached over a railing and struck him with a stun cane. The man was later arrested. (November 2016)

As **Sam Smith** worked in his yard, a female neighbor approached. "She began using racial slurs and then saying she checked with the whole neighborhood, who say that they don't want me here and that I should do everybody a favor and just leave." Smith called authorities to lodge a complaint, and officers spoke to the woman, who admitted admitted to using the n-word. The woman's husband arrived and threatened in front of police to "kick Smith's ass." The next day, Smith found the window of his truck broken out. When he had originally inquired about the house, he was told more than once that it was sold; he had been able to make the purchase only by having a White friend make the deal. (August 2015)

DARRIEN HUNT (22) was shot dead by officers responding to a report of a suspicious person walking around with a "samurai-type" sword. The sword was a toy replica that Hunt wore slung over his shoulder. Officers claimed they fired because Hunt brandished the sword and lunged at them, but Hunt was, in fact, shot in the back six times as he fled, as corroborated by witnesses. The officers faced no charges. (September 2014)

A White man wrote a letter to a White couple who had taken in a Black child. Among other things, the letter stated: "I catch that nigger around my daughter I'll kill the asshole and then go find what stupid person brought him here in the first place." It concluded with the line "Get this nigger out!" The man was arrested, fined, and sentenced to a year in prison. (December 2013)

Local Resources

American Civil Liberties Union of Utah: acluutah.org, (801) 521-9862
Utah NAACP: naacptristateinu.org, (801) 250-5088;
naacp-saltlakebranch.org
Utah Department of Human Services: hs.utah.gov/civil-rights/

VERMONT
1.3% Black
(about 8,000 out of 624,000)

	Black	White
Poverty Rate	n/a	10%
Unemployment Rate	n/a	3.6%
Imprisonment Ratio	10.5	1

Open carry permitted: YES	Stand your ground law: NO
Active hate groups: 1	2016 election result: Democrat

VERMONT (Cont.)

Percentage of Black victims of law enforcement killings (2013-16):
0%
(0 out of 5)

Notable Incidents

Burlington High School students at a football game hurled racial slurs during a fight. In a separate incident at the same game, a student from the visiting school brought a sign characterizing Black players as convicts and gang members. (September 2016)

In response to **Kiah Morris** winning re-election as a local state representative, a man sent her a message on Twitter that included a caricature of a Black person and the caption, "Sheeeit, I be representin dem white muhfugguhz of Bennington, gnome sayin?" The man, who identifies as an alt-right movement and White nationalism supporter, sent additional messages and initiated an in-person encounter, prompting issuance of a restraining order. (August 2016)

Shortly after a Black couple in a northern Vermont college community put a Black Lives Matter sign in their yard, a dead and bloodied black cat in a bag was placed on their property. A few days later, they found that their locks had been tampered with. They moved away in response. (December 2015)

A man who claimed to be a recruiter distributed KKK fliers bearing an image of a horse-mounted Klansman holding a burning cross. **Jocellyn Harvey** and another recipient of color contacted authorities. (October 2015)

Local Resources

American Civil Liberties Union of Vermont: acluvt.org, (802) 223-6304
VT Human Rights Commission: http: hrc.vermont.gov, (800) 416-2010
Vermont NAACP:
champlainareanaacp.wixsite.com/champlain-area-naacp

VIRGINIA
19.7% Black
(about 1,600,000 out of 8,400,000)

	Black	White
Poverty Rate	21%	7%
Unemployment Rate	6.7%	3.3%
Imprisonment Ratio	5	1

Open carry permitted: YES	Stand your ground law: NO
Active hate groups: 21	2016 election result: Democrat

Percentage of Black victims of law enforcement killings (2013-16):
43.7%
(31 out of 71)

Notable Incidents

A little league complex was vandalized with swastikas, insults to members of the Black Lives Matter movement, and the words "White Power." (December 2016)

After being asked by **Ricky Berry** and his roommate **Philip Blackwell** if sliced cheese was available for purchase, employees at a CVS hid in an office and called the police to report the men as suspicious persons. An officer arrived and Berry and Blackwell were asked to leave. (November 2016)

A historic one-room schoolhouse that had served Black children during segregation was covered with spray-painted swastikas and racist messages, including the words "White Power." Local students had been working to convert the building into a museum. (October 2016)

White firefighters refused to provide **Stacey Claiborne** with a small amount of ice to help her stop her 11-year-old son's nosebleed. The initial denial turned into seven minutes of questioning, while her son's nose continued to bleed, until she decided to forego hope of assistance. (August 2016)

Thirteen-year-old **Za'Khari Waddy** wrote and delivered the following letter to his school's administration:

To Whom It May Concern: Yesterday on the football bus coming from our football game a kid ... started saying racist things to me. He then started saying he does not like blacks and he told me 200 years ago my ancestors hung from a tree and after he said that I should I hang from a tree. That made me super mad, so in the locker room I told him not to call me n----r or that I should be hung on a tree. The coaches took me away from the kid because I was really mad and they think I was going to fight him but I want someone to do something about it because I'm tired of boys messing with me because of my skin. I'm at my boiling point with this. Please do something about this because when I bring it to the office/principle [sic] you do nothing about it and I'm tired of the racism.

(October 2015)

A Black delivery driver for a

Lowe's store, **Marcus Bradley**, was recalled from a delivery. Upon inquiring why, he was told that the customer had requested that the delivery person not be Black. A reporter contacted the customer, who confirmed her request, stating, "I got a right to have whatever I want and that's it." (August 2015)

> **I'm not talking to you, you black nigger.**
> —n e i g h b o r

WILLIAM CHAPMAN (18) was confronted in a Walmart parking lot by a police officer who had been called for a suspected shoplifter. According to a security guard who witnessed the encounter, Chapman did defy orders, at which point a struggle ensued. Chapman broke free, and the officer pulled his gun. Chapman, who was unarmed, responded to this by saying, "Are you going to fucking shoot me?" and making a "fighting gesture," according to the witness, who clarified: "He never charged. It was basically a jab step." The officer then shot Chapman twice from several feet away. He was subsequently indicted and found guilty of first degree murder. (April 2015)

University of Virginia student **Martese Johnson** writes: "On the night of March 18, 2015, three white Alcoholic Beverage Control officers asked me for identification outside of a bar adjacent to the University of Virginia's grounds. I showed them my I.D., which they wrongly assumed was a fake I.D. After a brief interaction with these officers, I was slammed to the ground violently, detained with handcuffs and leg shackles, and arrested without justification." Johnson was arrested on charges of resisting arrest and obstructing justice despite multiple accounts that, when confronted, Johnson did not resist arrest and was beaten despite his cooperation and bystanders' pleas for the officers to stop. (March 2015)

Fliers from the Loyal White Knights of the Ku Klux Klan were left on doorsteps in multiple areas. (January 2015 and April 2014)

Fliers from the Traditionalist American Knights of the Ku Klux Klan were left in driveways of residences. (March 2014)

A White mother in Virginia made a full Ku Klux Klan outfit for her 7-year-old son to wear for Halloween. When news media inquired, she stated that her brother had done the same as a child and that she had no issue with the Klan, which she said still exists in her town. She explained, "It's supposed to be white with white, black with black, man with woman and all of that. That's what the KKK stands for." (October 2013)

Fliers from the Loyal White Knights of the Ku Klux Klan were left in driveways. (August 2013)

A 12-year-old African-American boy was setting up a lemonade stand in the courtyard of a Fairfax, VA apartment complex when a person wearing a "Halloween-type" costume struck him with a urine-filled balloon, yelling "Go back to Africa, you nigger!" (July 2013)

Local Resources

American Civil Liberties Union of Virginia: acluva.org, (804) 644-8022
Attorney General, Division of Human Rights: oag.state.va.us/programs-initiatives/human-rights, (804) 225-2292
Virginia NAACP: vscnaacp.org

WASHINGTON
4.1% Black
(about 299,000 out of 7,300,000)

	Black	White
Poverty Rate	n/a	9%
Unemployment Rate	n/a	4.9%
Imprisonment Ratio	5.7	1

Open carry permitted: NO	Stand your ground law: NO
Active hate groups: 13	2016 election result: Democrat

Percentage of Black victims of law enforcement killings (2013-16):
10.3%
(12 out of 116)

Notable Incidents

The word "Niggers" was spray-painted on Spokane's Martin Luther King, Jr. Family Outreach Center. (November 2016)

A Native woman, Sharlaine LaClair, was bombarded with racist text messages and death threats during her candidacy for the State House of Representatives. Texts included:

- "Eat shit and die you inbred piece of nigger shit."
- "...if Donald wins your nigger ass is going into an oven! Legally."
- At one point the sender referred to LaClair's son as a "dumb piece of nigger shit."
- The author threatened to castrate "every nigger" if Clinton won the election. The man who sent the messages was convicted of a

hate crime. (October 2016)

While out of town, the family home and vehicle of **Marvin Phillips** were covered in racist graffiti. "I was told it was graffiti and nobody wanted to say what it really was," said Phillips. "They finally said, 'Marvin, it was the n-word and KKK, stuff like that.'" The town banded together to clean and paint away the vandalism. (August 2016)

Upon seeing a Black man and White woman kiss, a White supremacist male approached the couple, yelled a racial slur, and lunged with a knife, grazing the woman and stabbing the man in the hip. Upon the assailant's capture, he said, "Yeah, I stabbed them; I'm a white supremacist" and began talking about Donald Trump rallies and attacking people at a Black Lives Matter protest. His tattoos included the words "skinhead" and "white power" as well as an image of the Confederate flag. (August 2016)

> Yall Black ppl better start picking yall slave numbers.
> —HIGH SCHOOL GRAFFITI

A White woman with two biracial children found a letter on her porch that read as follows:

> I AM SICK AND TIRED OF THIS BULLSHIT. YOU NEED TO GET YOUR NIGGER LOVING ASS OUT OF HERE, AND ALL THESE BLACK LIVES MATTER BULLSHIT. YOU FUCKING AROUND AND TEARING UP OUR RACE HAVING ALL THESE NIGGER BABIES. FUCKING NIGGER LOVER!!!! U AND ALL THESE NIGGERS NEED TO LEAVE THIS COUNTRY THAT'S OURS! ONE DAY YOUR KIDS WILL GET WHAT THEY DESERVE BEING ON THIS LAND. FUCKING NIGGER LOVERS!!!!!!!!!!! WHITE LIVES MATTER

FUCKING NIGGER LOVERS!!! GO TRUMP!!! (July 2016)

A predominantly Black church in Seattle was burglarized, ransacked, and defaced. Graffiti included the words "Go back 2 Africa," swastikas, and the word "nigger." (April 2016)

Five members of Whitworth University's women's soccer team were suspended from a game after a picture of them wearing costumes with blackface to an unofficial team event went viral. (September 2015)

A White supremacist group called Volksfront was planning a rally in support of the police, who had just shot **Bryson Tyler Chaplin** and **Andre Damon Thompson** after a shoplifting incident. Chaplin and Thompson had gotten caught trying to steal beer from a grocery store and fled. The police were called, and both men, who were unarmed, were shot. Counter-protestors sought out the Volksfront rally, and both sides clashed physically. (May 2015)

Fliers from the Traditionalist American Knights of the Ku Klux Klan were left in driveways. (March 2015)

A package of racist, threatening literature was sent to the president of the local chapter of the NAACP. (February 2015)

A White Phi Delta Theta fraternity member was expelled from the organization after using a racial slur against a group of young Black women at Washington State University. (February 2015)

As **Raymond Wilford** walked past an Israeli occupation protest at a mall, a shirtless White man who had been berating protestors incited an altercation by spitting on him. A White security guard intervened with pepper spray drawn and pointed at Wilford, who asked, "Why are you pointing mace at me? He's the one being aggressive." The security guard then pepper-sprayed Wilford, and the White antagonist fled. Bystander video shows that, despite myriad eyewitnesses all pointing out that he had the wrong party, the guard manhandled, handcuffed, and detained Wilford anyway. (August 2014)

A White female police officer accosted and arrested **William Wingate** (70) for using a golf club as a walking cane. The officer accused him of swinging the golf club at her while she was driving, despite dashcam footage completely to the contrary, and stated in court that she had considered using lethal force against him. She was subsequently fired. (July 2014)

A trio of White teenagers, one of whom was the babysitter, robbed a White family's home and blamed it on two armed Black males. Next-door-neighbor **Cody Oaks** was arrested at gunpoint for the crime until the 4-year-old daughter of the family that was robbed told police that the crime had been committed by men with "peach-colored skin" rather than "dark-colored skin." (June 2014)

Fifteen-year-old **Monique Tillman** and her brother were bicycling home through a mall parking lot when two White security officers, one of whom was an off-duty cop, pursued them and accused them of trespassing. When Tillman made a move as if to leave, the officer yanked her from the bike, slammed her against a car, choked her, snatched her by the hair, and tased her. The encounter was captured on surveillance video. Tillman was arrested and charged with resisting arrest and assault on an officer, charges that were dismissed by the court. A lawsuit is pending against the officer, the security company, and the mall. (May 2014)

Local Resources

American Civil Liberties Union of Washington: aclu-wa.org
Washington NAACP: naacpaowsac.org
WA State Human Rights Commission: hum.wa.gov, (800) 233-3247

WEST VIRGINIA
3.6% Black
(about 66,000 out of 1,800,000)

	Black	White
Poverty Rate	25%	14%
Unemployment Rate	n/a	6.7%
Imprisonment Ratio	3.5	1

Open carry permitted: YES	Stand your ground law: YES
Active hate groups: 4	2016 election result: Republican

Percentage of Black victims of law enforcement killings (2013-16):
9.5%
(4 out of 42)

Notable Incidents

JAMES MEANS (15) was shot to death by a 62-year-old White man who later stated, "the way I look at it, that's another piece of trash off the street." Eyewitness testimony and video footage confirm that the teenager had a BB gun in his waistband but nothing in his hands when the elder man shot him—once in the chest and once in the back—after they bumped into each other and had a prolonged exchange of words. The man claimed he felt "threatened" despite audio of the incident confirming that he knew the teenager's gun was a toy. (November 2016)

After the election, a White woman residing in Clay, WV posted on Facebook that "It will be so refreshing to have a classy, beautiful, dignified First Lady back in the White House. I'm tired of seeing an ape in heels." The mayor, also a White woman, replied: "Just made my day, Pam." The mayor ultimately resigned, and the woman who made the post was suspended and later fired. (November 2016)

An elementary school teacher's aide was suspended for ten days without pay after using racial slurs in a Facebook post. (November 2016)

A spokeswoman for the West Virginia attorney general's office was fired after her participation in "THE 'Stop White Genocide' Video" was discovered. In the infamous video, the woman repeatedly states, "anti-racist is a code word for anti-white," a well-known phrase coined by notorious White supremacist Bob Whitaker. (August 2016)

GARRICK HOPKINS (60) and his brother, **CARL HOPKINS, JR.** (61), were inspecting an emptied shed on land they had purchased when the previous owner, a White man, decided they were breaking and entering and shot them dead with a rifle. (January 2014)

Fliers from the Loyal White Knights of the KKK were distributed in a neighborhood. (October 2013)

Local Resources

American Civil Liberties Union of West Virginia: acluwv.org
West Virginia Human Rights Commission: hrc.wv.gov, (304) 558-2616

WISCONSIN
6.6% Black
(about 381,000 out of 5,700,000)

	Black	White
Poverty Rate	20%	9%
Unemployment Rate	n/a	3.5%
Imprisonment Ratio	11.5	1

Open carry permitted: YES	Stand your ground law: NO
Active hate groups: 5	2016 election result: Republican

Percentage of Black victims of law enforcement killings (2013-16):
27.8%
(15 out of 54)

Notable Incidents

"Go Home Niggers" was written on the door of an off-campus residence shared by Black students of the University of Wisconsin at La Crosse. (November 2016)

Two mixed-race families that patronized the West Side Swim Club in Madison were the target of a hand-written hate letter that referred to them as "nigga lovers" and "race traitors." The letter also stated, "You and yours need to stay seperate [sic]—NOT EQUAL.

Your life isn't valuable to any of us. #DONT MATTER—stay out of Westside. OUT." It concludes, "TRUMP WON. Go home. Race wars are on! White powers, privelidge [sic] race traitors finish last. Signed, The World." (November 2016)

A University of Wisconsin at Madison fan was photographed at a football game wearing a President Obama mask with a noose attached. (October 2016)

University of Wisconsin at Madison police on Thursday pulled a Black student from class and arrested him for allegedly spray-painting anti-racist messages across campus. The arrest, which came at a time when the university was dealing with a number of racist incidents on campus, led more than 700 students, staff, and faculty members to sign a letter accusing the university and its police department of caring more about the graffiti than the issues to which the writings were drawing attention. (April 2016)

A high school student in Kenosha County wore a Ku Klux Klan costume to deliver an English class presentation. An outspoken biracial student at the school, **Mykah Simmons**, subsequently found the word "nigger" etched onto the top of her school desk. Simmons averred that, since starting the school that past year, she had been called Shaquita and nigger, among other slurs, had been physically accosted, and had been threatened with lynching. (April 2016)

Graffiti found at the University of Wisconsin at Madison consisted of a stick figure hanging from a tree by a noose and the N-word. (March 2016)

University of Wisconsin at Madison freshman **Synovia Knox** was arriving home with friends when her neighbor started shouting profanities and racially charged comments. He was "telling us we were poor and that we were on scholarship and we didn't even belong here," Knox explained. The student started to push Knox and her friends before using his chest to pin her against a wall and spitting in her face. (March 2016)

Think we should make slaves again. —VOLUNTEER FIREFIGHTER

Four-time elected sheriff of Milwaukee County, David A. Clarke, Jr.—who is Black—said the following on *Fox & Friends*: "First off, there is no police brutality in America. We ended that back in the '60s. There's a new Harvard study out that shows that there is no racism in the hearts of police officers. They go about their daily duty, if you will, to keep communities safe." Further, Clarke describes Black Lives Matter as "vile, vulgar, slimy," a "subversive" hate group, and a terrorist movement. (October 2015)

When Milwaukee Bucks player **John Henson** and a friend attempted to buy a Rolex at a local jewelry store, the staff hid in an office and called the police. (October 2015)

Graffiti of swastikas and the words "kill Obama now" was found on the side of a storage building. (January 2015)

A White man (Nathaniel Homestead) pointed a gun at a Madison police officer but was not shot. (December 2014)

DONTRE HAMILTON, who suffered from schizophrenia, had been reported to police as "a homeless guy sleeping" in the park. Two other officers had previously responded to the scene and determined no offense being committed. A third officer, who was White, accosted Hamilton, making him stand for a frisk, which resulted in Hamilton becoming combative. A struggle ensued, and the officer began striking Hamilton with his baton until Hamilton was able to procure it from him and land a blow with it. The officer then shot Hamilton 14 times. (April 2014)

Local Resources

American Civil Liberties Union of Wisconsin: aclu-wi.org, (414) 272-4032
Wisconsin NAACP: wi-naacp.org

WYOMING
1.4% Black
(about 8,000 out of 585,000)

	Black	White
Poverty Rate	n/a	9%
Unemployment Rate	n/a	3.9%
Imprisonment Ratio	3.5	1

Open carry permitted: YES	Stand your ground law: NO
Active hate groups: 2	2016 election result: Republican

Percentage of Black victims of law enforcement killings (2013-16):
0%
(0 out of 14)

Notable Incidents

A Black motorist, **Brandeon Guyton**, was having a phone conversation when a White man on a motorcycle yelled at him to "get off the phone and pay attention, nigger." Guyton then started recording the man, who, when asked to repeat himself, replied "fuck you, nigger." (August 2016)

A White woman became involved in an altercation with a Black woman, stabbing her three times as a result and calling her a "nigger." At trial, the White woman admitted using the slur and added that having done so made her feel "disgusted." (July 2016)

After overhearing two White men use the term "nigger," former Marine **Clayton Denny** confronted them. The conversation seemed to go well, but the men then followed him outside and beat him to the point that one of them thought he had been killed. They yelled racial slurs at him during the attack. The men claimed self-defense, but camera footage proved otherwise. (May 2016)

Local Resources

American Civil Liberties Union of Wyoming: aclu-wy.org
Wyoming NAACP: naacpstateconference.org, (844) UR-NAACP

DATA SOURCES

Population
https://www.census.gov/quickfacts/

Poverty
http://www.kff.org/other/state-indicator/poverty-rate-by-raceethnicity/

Unemployment
http://www.epi.org/publication/state-unemployment-rates-by-race-and-ethnicity-at-the-end-of-2015-show-a-plodding-recovery/

Imprisonment
http://www.sentencingproject.org/the-facts/#map

Open Carry
http://smartgunlaws.org/category/state-open-carrying-of-guns/

Stand Your Ground
http://criminal.findlaw.com/criminal-law-basics/states-that-have-stand-your-ground-laws.html
http://smartgunlaws.org/gun-laws/policy-areas/firearms-in-public-places/stand-your-ground-laws/

Hate Groups & Incidents
https://www.splcenter.org/hate-map
https://www.splcenter.org/fighting-hate/hate-incidents

Law Enforcement Killings
https://mappingpoliceviolence.org/states/

#SayTheirNames INDEX

Akai Gurley, 121
Alexander Wilson, 27
Alton Sterling, 77
Andrew Anthony Williams, 50
Anthony Hill, 58
Brandon Tate-Brown, 150
Brendon Glenn, 34
Calin Roquemore, 170
Cameron Massey, 23
Cameron Tillman, 80
Carl Hopkins, Jr., 188
Charles Goodridge, 173
Charly Keunang, 35
Christian Taylor, 172
Clementa C. Pinckney, 156
Corey Jones, 48
Craig McKinnis, 73
Cynthia Marie Graham-Hurd, 156
Dalvin Hollins, 25
Daniel Martin, 144
Daniel Simmons, 156
Darrien Hunt, 176
David Joseph, 170
David L. Robinson, 111

Deion Fludd, 123
DePayne Middleton-Doctor, 156
Deravis Caine Rogers, 56
Dontre Hamilton, 191
Emerson Crayton, Jr., 23
Eric Garner, 122
Eric Harris, 142
Ernest Satterwhite, 157
Ervin Edwards, 81
Ethel Lee Lance, 156
Ezell Ford, 36
Freddie Gray, 85
Garrick Hopkins, 188
Gregory Gunn, 22
James Means, 187
Jason Harrison, 173
Jeremey Lake, 143
Jeremy McDole, 45
Jermaine McBean, 53
Jessica Williams, 31
John Crawford III, 138
John T. Wilson III, 110
Jonathan Ferrell, 130
Jonathan Sanders, 96
Jordan Baker, 174
Kouren-Rodney Thomas, 127
Laquan McDonald, 65
Larry Jackson, Jr., 174
Michael Brown, 104
Michael Lee Marshall, 40
Michael Sabbie, 29
Michael Tingling, 67
Michelle Cusseaux, 26
Miriam Carey, 43

Myra Thompson, 156
Naeschylus Vinzant, 40
Philando Castile, 93
Phillip White, 115
Ray Anson Mitchell, 23
Renisha McBride, 92
Richard Gene Swihart, 31
Robert Storay, 29
Rumain Brisbon, 26
Samuel Dubose, 137
Samuel Harrell, 121
Sandra Bland, 172
Sharonda Coleman-Singleton, 156
Susie Jackson, 156
Tamir Rice, 138
Terence Crutcher, 141
Terrence Sterling, 43
Thomas Lane, 42
Tommy Yancy, Jr., 37
Toussaint Harrison, 38
Tywanza Sanders, 156
Walter Scott, 156
William Chapman, 181
William Sims, 30
Yvette Smith, 174
Zikarious Flint, 58

CPSIA information can be obtained
at www.ICGtesting.com
Printed in the USA
LVHW030753040319
609387LV00005B/563